NATURAL WONDERS
of the WORLD

NATURAL WONDERS
of the WORLD

P J Banyard

BOOK CLUB ASSOCIATES · London

*Half title page:
A 1,600-year-old
Arborvitae or Tree of
Life – the oldest and
largest of its kind in
the world. (Daily
Telegraph/Len Rhodes)*

*Title page: An Arctic
landscape. (Daily
Telegraph/Leo
Dickinson)*

*Endpapers:
A hurricane
photographed from
above.
(Orbis Publishing)*

© Orbis Publishing Limited,
London 1978
Printed in Great Britain by
Colorgraphic Ltd., Leicester
This edition published 1979
by Book Club Associates,
by arrangement with
Orbis Publishing Limited
ISBN: 0 85613 480 5

Contents

Left: Autumn in the
American Rocky
Mountains.
(Bruce Coleman)

Introduction

Once there was nothing. There was no space and there was no time. Then, between 13 and 18 billion years ago, all the primeval matter which makes up the universe burst out from another dimension and exploded. Ever since the blast this matter has continued to rush outwards so that the universe is constantly expanding. This expansion may go on for ever, but there is new evidence that it is slowing down and that the forces of gravity will prevail and pull all matter back to its point of origin to form a dense mass until another explosion sends it outwards again. It is possible that the universe undergoes 100 billion-year cycles of alternate expansion and contraction and there is no way of knowing how many have occurred before the present one.

As a result of the great explosion which began the creation of our planet there are billions of star groups, known as galaxies, flying away from each other. In the vast reaches of our galaxy alone there are something like 100 billion to 200 billion stars. Our galaxy – the uninspiringly named Milky Way – is a spiral galaxy and consists of a disc-shaped mass around a spherical centre. The stars of the Milky Way are greatly varied in size and strength with the biggest stars being hundreds of thousands of times bigger than the smallest and the hottest stars one hundred times hotter than the coolest. There is a rather cool average-sized star near the central plane of the galaxy and that insignificant-seeming speck amid the heavenly bodies is of vital importance to us because it is our sun. Orbiting around the sun are various planets and one of the nearer of these is planet Earth. The scale of this is more comprehensible when it is reduced to familiar proportions: if the sun were the size of a football, Earth would be the size of a pinhead and located 24.69 metres (81 feet) away. On this scale the nearest star – apart from the sun – would be some 6,400 kilometres (4,000 miles) away which gives some idea of the staggering distances involved.

But our solar system, which consists of the sun, 9 planets, 31 moons, more than 30,000 asteroids and countless comets and dust particles, was not created in the original great explosion that sent the galaxies hurtling on their way. Somewhere along the journey of the Milky Way our solar system began to form from a 'cloud' of dispersed hydrogen and other matter – the existence of such clouds in space can be recognized today because they impede the passage of light from behind them. Two of the fundamental properties of matter seem to be gravitational attraction and rotation of mass. Gravity is simply the force of attraction between every particle of matter in the universe, and it increases in proportion to the number and type of particles in any particular body – in other words a football in space will exert some gravitational force but it will be incomparably smaller than the force exerted by the Earth. Gravitational force decreases with distance. Rotation is something which seems to affect all heavenly bodies: the Earth rotates, the sun rotates and even the galaxy rotates. The solar system began when pressure of light on a certain hydrogen cloud caused the hydrogen to conglomerate. The conglomeration began to exert the pull of gravity and draw in more and more material and then, as it became an entity, the whole mass began to rotate.

As the material which was our solar system rotated it was affected by the conflicting forces of gravity and the centrifugal

Right: Planet Earth photographed from space. The basic division of the Earth's crust between continents and oceans is strikingly apparent and the outlines of Africa and Arabia are just discernible. The Arctic and Antarctic ice caps are visible and cloud systems circulate in the atmosphere.

force outwards from the centre of rotation. These two forces caused the matter to divide up and while most of it remained in a central blob, which was to become the sun, other blobs began to form at a distance from it and to enlarge as their own gravity increased and they swept up spacial debris of frozen gases and meteorites. These outer blobs of matter were to become the planets and the whole process took place in darkness and at low temperatures. This evolution of planets seems rather complex and unlikely, but nevertheless it is a generally accepted theory. The idea is more easily grasped when one watches a demonstration model of a mass of floating, magnetic balls which are revolved over water. As the balls are revolved some of them will be spun away from the central mass and then conglomerate at various distances from it.

The planets which separated from the sun were much larger than they are now and, like the sun, they were composed principally of hydrogen although a small percentage of their mass was composed of heavier elements – the spacial rubble perhaps of some dead and long exploded star of the past. This rubble of different elements amid the hydrogen was of great importance to the creation of the solar system because, although it is theoretically possible for the separate elements to have been constructed by hydrogen fusion during the formation of the sun and its planets, it is much more likely that they were created in very dense stars at temperatures of many millions of degrees. Whatever the origin of the various elements, gravitational pressures caused them to separate so that the heaviest elements concentrated at each planet's core. As gravitational energy began to work on the vast mass of the sun, it con-

verted to heat and fusion of the hydrogen atoms began. New elements were formed and the sun began to give off light, heat and sub-atomic particles. This solar wind of particles swept the planets and carried off most of their lighter, gaseous components so that only the heavier elements remained.

Meanwhile, the pressure of gravity had concentrated the heaviest elements – such as iron – at the centre of the Earth. This compression and separation of elements may have occurred very rapidly and caused the Earth to become molten or it may have occurred slowly so that melting only happened later due to the decay of radioactive elements. The point is that, at some stage, the Earth did become molten and lighter elements floated out from the molten core and cooled forming a thin crust about four billion years ago. This crust was and is somewhat varied. The lightest elements floated outwards above everything else to form the granitic rocks of the continents. The lower layer of the crust was formed with a greater proportion of the heavier elements and now underlies the continental crust and also forms the ocean floors.

The oceans themselves only developed later when the cooling of the crust enabled water to accumulate. This water came from the interior of the Earth and was carried to the surface as light water vapour. There is evidence from the sediments that they have left that seas and oceans have existed for at least three billion years.

This sequence of events, which led to the creation of the Earth is not proven beyond doubt, and indeed there is no theory as yet which offers an acceptable explanation to everybody. However, with the formation of the crust and the appearance of continents

Above: These contrasting dripstone decorations are found in a chamber of Shatter Cave in the English Mendips. A beautiful curtain of calcite can be seen on the left.

at the rate of a few centimetres a year, individual pieces or 'plates' of the Earth's crust may have wandered all over the globe. In geological terms, the familiar face of our planet with its present continents and oceans has only recently been achieved while the constant movements which alter their positions continue today.

So it is not a dead and static globe but a living, changing one. All the wonderful and strange phenomena mentioned in this book are part of this story of change and of the history of Earth's evolution. However dramatic and freakish some of them seem, they are all the natural product of the unique environment of this particular planet in its insignificant solar system amid the unimaginably vast reaches of space. To find out exactly which forces created each wonder of the world one has to delve into the history of the Earth and the laws of physics. The natural wonders selected for this anthology are not always described simply because of their great size, although some, such as Mount Everest or the Grand Canyon, are immediately included by virtue of their sheer unsurpassable scale. Anything that is unusual because of its size is probably well enough known in this modern age of mass communications. Many lesser known wonders, however, such as the pools of Keli Mutu or the Venus flytrap, are in this book because they are striking or extraordinary and because they repay a little investigation. It is probable that there are many more fascinating phenomena yet to be discovered in remote parts of the world, and it is the curiosity which nature's most bizarre and beautiful manifestations have always aroused that continues to stimulate the growth of knowledge about our planet.

and oceans, planet Earth was acquiring its familiar form. Vast changes were still to take place. Convection currents, which circulate within Earth's still semi-molten inner layers, continuously and slowly move great sections of the outer crust away from each other, towards each other and past each other. This process is very gradual but it has certainly been going on for 300 million years and possibly for 3,000 million years so that, even

THE
EARTH'S
SURFACE

Previous page:
Battlements of rock jut out in futile defiance of ceaseless attack by wind and rain. The floor of this wadi in the Band-i-Amir region of Afghanistan is covered in saline deposits left by evaporated water.

We tend to think that landscape is unchanging. We realize that our view of it may be changed – forests may be felled, motorways built and housing estates constructed – but the shape of the Earth with its ridges and valleys seems immutable. Yet vast changes have occurred and are still occurring to alter the familiar surface of the land. Over the aeons since the Earth's crust formed, continents have shifted about the globe, seas have come and gone, great chains of mountains have been raised and then worn down through erosion while the polar ice caps have advanced and retreated thousands of kilometres.

It is not only the small, everyday features that have been changed beyond recognition by their long history but the big picture – the map of the world's continents – has been transformed over the ages. There was no Atlantic Ocean 250 million years ago when South America, Antarctica, Australia, India and Africa all formed part of one large continent which geologists have named Pangaea. At the same time North America, Greenland and Eurasia were also joined together. About 225 million years ago Pangaea broke up and the continents moved away from each other at the rate of a few centimetres a year to take up their present positions. The mechanisms which propel them – for they are still moving – are the slow convection currents which rise from the molten core of the Earth. The Earth's surface is divided up into a half-dozen major pieces or plates and a number of smaller ones. These plates are not broken up but remain cohesive as they are pushed slowly away from each other or towards each other by the convection currents below them. Obviously this continuous process has produced vast alterations to the physical appearance of our planet over millions of years.

This slow movement of plates about the Earth is also responsible for the raising of great chains of mountains. Where plates collide – as the South American plate is colliding with a Pacific Ocean plate – the thinner oceanic crust is forced down beneath the thicker, lighter continental crust but the continental crust is folded and deformed by this. In South America this de-

formation has resulted in raising the Andes chain of mountains – which is still growing. On the occasions when continental crust has collided directly with more continental crust, neither plate can be forced down by the other and so they converge to a crumpled and thickened zone of the crust – such earth movements have raised the exceptionally high ranges of the Himalayas which culminate in the ultimate peak of Everest. Smaller, isolated lumps and mountains have been raised upon the Earth's surface by volcanism, and Mount Fuji in Japan is an excellent example of this.

Over the ages this mountain-building has been counterbalanced by the remorseless attack of erosion. It is difficult to imagine the destructive effect that wind and weather can have on soaring peaks of solid rock because a human generation has such a short timespan in geological terms. But, over millions of years, great mountain ranges have been worn flat by the constant friction of wind and rain – the Musgrave range of central Australia was once 4,600 metres (15,000 feet) but now reaches only about 920 metres

(3,000 feet) above the surrounding plain where it overlooks the eerie solitude of Ayers Rock. The awesome scouring performed by rivers is most obviously illustrated by the Grand Canyon which has been cut out to a depth of 1,500 metres (5,000 feet) by the Colorado river. The sediment that is carried away by the water is not destroyed but becomes sedimentary rock such as sandstone when it reaches the end of its journey. In time earth movements may thrust up the sandstone, which lies at the bottom of a sea, so that it is once again exposed to weathering where it has produced such extraordinary outcrops as the Stone Towers of Arizona. And, as well as all the work by rivers, there is yet more erosion by underground water, wind and powerful glaciers – to form yet more fabulous features of the landscape such as limestone caves, desert dunes and mountain fjords.

With all these influences at work the Earth's surface is constantly changing. The natural wonders of the Earth are dramatic illustrations of the impermanence of anything over the aeons of geological time.

Above: A view across the gigantic Ngorongoro crater in Tanzania. These superb vistas have their origins aeons ago in great earth movements and subsequent erosion by wind and rain.

The Grand Canyon

The Grand Canyon is a deep gorge cut from the Colorado Plateau by the Colorado river. It is beautiful and mysterious, the result of a combination of unusual and improbable natural events. J. B. Priestley said of it: 'I have heard rumours of visitors who were disappointed. The same people will be disappointed at the day of judgment.' The day of judgment will no doubt loom larger when it comes, but the Grand Canyon nevertheless provides an unforgettable sight.

The first white people to visit the Canyon are thought to have been the members of the Coronado expedition of 1540, and two Spanish priests rediscovered it in 1776. Beaver trappers examined it after this and members of American government expeditions exploring the Wild West looked it over. But the first important expedition down the Canyon was led by John Wesley Powell and his companions in 1869, and again in 1870. They descended the Colorado river in rowboats and produced reports on the geography, geology and ethnology of the area.

Powell was very impressed with the Canyon though his or any other written description, or indeed any photograph, can hardly do justice to the spectacle presented by the Canyon. A recitation of facts and statistics, however, is enough to stir the imagination. It is 1200 to 1500 metres (4–5000 feet) deep from its more or less horizontal rims, from six to twenty-eight kilometres (four to eighteen miles) wide at the top, and 354 kilometres (220 miles) long. It is a great gash in the Plateau cut by the Colorado river to such a depth that the Canyon walls expose rocks of various strata and age in a number of colours. This rich range of colours made John Wesley Powell

Right: A view from the lip of the Grand Canyon. It gives an idea of the deep groove that the Colorado river has cut through a hard rock bed.

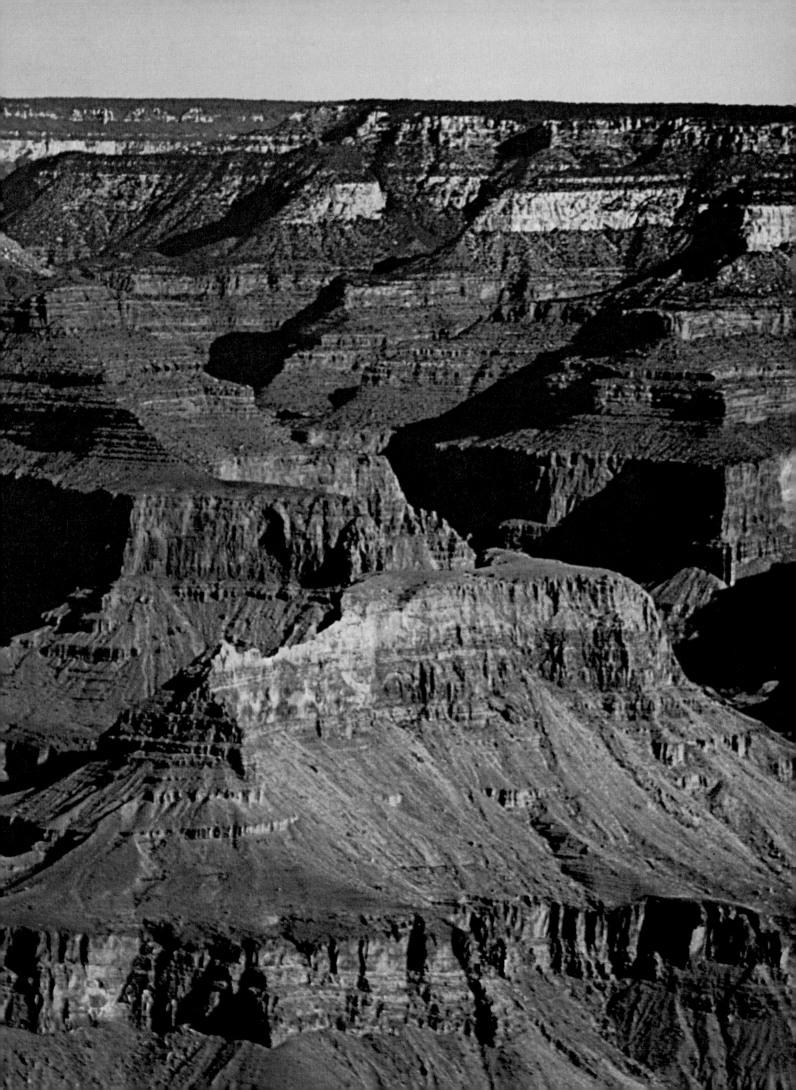

exclaim that the Grand Canyon was 'the most sublime spectacle on the Earth'.

It was Powell, too, who told of the Indian legend of the Canyon which gives a romantic account of its origins.

'Long ago, there was a great wise chief, who mourned the death of his wife, and would not be comforted until Ta-vwoats, one of the Indian gods came to him and offered to take him to see her in a happier land, if, upon his return, he would cease to mourn. The Great Chief promised. Then Ta-vwoats made a trail through the mountains that intervene between that beautiful land, the balmy region in the great west, and this the desert home of the poor Nu-ma. This trail was the canyon gorge of the Colorado. Through it he led him; and, when they had returned, the deity extracted from the chief a promise that he would tell no one of the joys of the land, lest, through discontent with the circumstances of this world, they should desire to go to heaven. Then he rolled a river into the gorge, a mad, raging stream,

that should engulf any that might attempt to enter thereby.'

Numerous Indian tribes once lived around the Grand Canyon and even today the ruins of ancient cliff-dwelling can be seen locally as well as the remarkable villages of the Pueblo Indians who still maintain their unique traditions in north-eastern Arizona and western New Mexico. The Pueblo tribes live in permanent village communities, in houses made of adobe-covered wood and stone, arranged around a central plaza which provides the venue for social and ceremonial events. Pueblo culture is about a thousand years old and they have always had a highly developed agricultural economy, farming semi-desert land by means of sophisticated irrigation techniques and growing crops of corn, beans, squashes, cotton, gourds and tobacco. They played an important role in the introduction of the horse to other Indian tribes although shrewdly they themselves did not become dependent on the horse in contrast with other nomadic Indian tribes who relied on the less stable rewards of

Above: This sinuous curve in the Grand Canyon shows that the Colorado river did not cut a straight course. This is remarkable because it is usually only sluggish rivers which meander and swift-running streams tend to run straighter.

hunting and gathering. The Pueblo peoples were better able than most Indian tribes to resist white intrusions into their communities. The land they cultivated was too arid to be attractive to the first settlers and the ethic of collective responsibility engendered by the agricultural community gave them an unusually strong sense of identity. Their villages can still be seen near the Canyon today and the Pueblo heritage is maintained by some twenty distinct clans.

The Indian description of the Colorado as a mad, raging stream is still fair today. The Colorado certainly needs to flow at speeds of almost 32 kmph (20 mph) to carve such a deep channel for itself. The present lie of the land makes the Canyon an unlikely choice as the course of the Colorado for, if the great Canyon had not been cut, the river would be flowing uphill. Geologists normally explain this by claiming that the lie of the land altered about a million years ago and the plateau began rising slowly. As the land rose the river was able to cut down into it and maintain its original course.

This theory does not satisfy everyone, however, because the bottom of the Canyon is cut through some very hard and ancient rock. To cut so deep and so quickly a river would have to be an almost unimaginable torrent, dragging abrasive silt and rocks in its swirling waters. This sort of river would have had to carry a great deal more water than it does today. Some geologists contend that melt-water from great glaciers at the end of the various ice ages and rainwater from the wet or pluvial periods of the Earth's history could have turned the Colorado into the sort of swollen, rock-scouring flood necessary to cut the Grand Canyon. Other geologists maintain that the

rocks of the Colorado Plateau show that the pluvial periods were never very wet in this area and that melting glaciers could never have made a big enough contribution to the river waters. They maintain that the plateau began to rise not one million but possibly 50 million years ago.

One must leave the argument with the experts who still argue the time-scale to the formation of this vast natural phenomenon which has continually impressed scientists and spectators alike. In the words of the famous geologist, F. E. Matthes, 'the alpine mountain ranges of this country are equalled and exceeded in height, if not in spectacular beauty, by those of other lands, but though there are elsewhere deep canyons, some of even greater depth than the Grand Canyon of the Colorado, there is not one that can match its vastness, its majesty, its ornate sculpture, and its wealth of color. Whoever stands upon the brink of the Grand Canyon beholds a spectacle unrivaled on this earth.' Matthes' testimony still holds as anyone visiting the Grand Canyon would confirm.

Above: Although the exposed rocks in the Grand Canyon look bare and inhospitable, they harbour various forms of animal and plant life.

The Balancing Rocks of the Matopos Hills

In Rhodesia's Matopos Hills there are crazy, toppling towers of stacked rocks. In other parts of the world, odd rocks, some of them of great size, can be found balancing precariously in unlikely places but they are seldom balancing on a tier of other rocks looking as though they might be blown over by a strong wind. Yet this strange structure occurs again and again in the lovely, wild setting of the Matopos. There is something so extravagant and improbable about these stone cairns that they appear almost as though they were erected by man. This is the area, unique in sub-Saharan Africa, in which ancient pre-colonial stone buildings have been found. More than 100 such sites have been located in this granite-rich area and possibly their architects were inspired by, and consciously imitated, the extraordinary natural edifices that surrounded them. No doubt the availability of local granite for building purposes encouraged such enterprise and ensured the preservation of these ancient stone complexes, unique to this part of Africa. The masons who constructed Great Zimbabwe, however, never had any part in shaping the balancing rocks of the Matopos which were positioned by a perfectly straightforward natural process.

Boulders are often found in odd places because they were carried along by glaciers and then left high and dry when the glaciers retreated at the end of the Ice Age. But ice does not pile boulders in columns. The Rhodesian rocks were formed by the simple processes of weathering and erosion. The Matopos Hills are granite outcrops. Granite is an igneous rock – that is to say one which was originally a molten magma. When it cooled and solidified, deep down beneath the surface, it developed great fractures which now help to control the shape of the huge dome-shaped hills, and some of them, much more closely spaced, later formed the balancing rocks.

Eventually the process of erosion brought the surface down to the top layer of granite blocks. Once exposed to the rain the cracks between the blocks became channels for the water which decomposed some of the mineral grains of the granite and wore it away. The result of this was that the rocks became more separated and their corners more rounded. During the day the sun warmed the outcrop and it expanded, while during the night it cooled. All this expanding and contracting caused an outside shell of rock to slab off. The fracture between the top shell of granite and the rest, however, was curved so that this process of slabbing-off or exfoliation meant that the rock shape became even more rounded. Where the granite blocks were a great size and only the top of them was exposed, this resulted in a typical 'whale-backed' hill. When the blocks were very much smaller and many of them had emerged, a pile of toppling, balancing rocks occurred.

This constantly repeated rock formation does not make the Matopos dull or unvaried. Indeed, their chief characteristic is a wild, rugged turbulence of shape and a very definite and beguiling atmosphere. They have long been fascinating to man. Their caves contain the beautiful drawings of the Bushmen, which show an astonishingly high level of technical competence, beside the less aesthetically satisfying doodles of the Bantu herdsmen. The wild terrain of the Matopos is so difficult and confusing that it was used by the warlike Matabele tribe as a last refuge in time of trouble. This time came

in 1896 when they had been severely defeated by a British force and its African levies led by Colonel (later Field Marshal and Lord) Plumer and following the great scout himself – Colonel Baden-Powell. In later years Plumer attained a certain sombre distinction as the British general who made fewest mistakes in the 1914–1918 war, but he could not beat the Matabele in their stronghold of the Matopos. Their fierce resistance amid these forbidding hills left them unvanquished and won them a peace settlement.

The chief reason for the fame of the Matopos, however, is that they are a burial-ground for the great and powerful. The dramatic effect of the granite architecture together with the presence of black eagles, believed to be the guardians of departed spirits, wheeling endlessly in the sky, have made them a setting for an important Bantu shrine. In 1868 the great King Mzilikazi, whose Nguni warriors had overrun Rhodesia, was buried in the Matopos in a noble sepulcore.

Less than fifty years later the body of one of the most powerful and forceful of self-made men was interred in the same hills. Cecil Rhodes, who amassed vast riches and built an empire for Queen Victoria in southern Africa, was laid to rest on the crown of Malindidzimu Hill where he had what he described as 'a view of the world'. There can be no greater indication of the enormous attraction of the granite hills with their strange balancing rocks than that they were chosen as the setting for monuments to a conquering warlord and a much travelled empire builder who could have picked any other place he wanted across two continents.

Left: The balancing rocks of the Matopos Hills. It seems as if a slight push would topple them, yet they have stood for millennia.

Mount Everest

At 8,848 metres (29,028 feet) the peak of Mount Everest is the highest point on the globe. This was discovered to be so as recently as 1852 and the mountain was then named after Sir George Everest, Surveyor-General in India from 1830 to 1843. The old Tibetan name Chomolungma was not known to western geographers at the time and so the world's greatest and most famous mountain is still internationally known by the name of a British official. The mountain is part of the Himalayas which form the highest range on Earth and one of the most inaccessible. Naturally the supreme target – Everest itself – has proved a magnet to climbers and many lives and much money have been spent on attempts to conquer it. Everest has proved to be more than a statistical ultimate or simply a high hill but a dangerous, difficult and fascinating mountain with a brooding presence worthy of its fame and pre-eminence. It was first climbed on 29 May 1953 and since then several other expeditions have managed to put people on the summit. In a sense the mountain remains unconquered as it is still capable of defeating the most carefully prepared expeditions equipped with every modern aid.

The inhabitants of the Himalayas think of them as the home and throne of the gods. To them Everest is Chomolungma, the goddess mother of the land. In their mythology the mountains are the oldest descendants of Prajapati, god of creation and roughly equivalent to Saturn in the Roman pantheon. In the beginning the mountains had wings and flew about settling where they pleased. Indra, the omnipotent god, whose role is roughly equivalent to that of the Roman Jupiter, cut off their wings

Left: The sheer incline of Mount Everest's south-western angle.
Overleaf: Only one climbing expedition is allowed to attempt Mount Everest at a time, and would-be climbers face a waiting list stretching to 1985.

and used them to stabilize heaven and Earth. The wings still hover about the mountain tops in the shape of storm clouds. So the ruthless Indra was the true creator of the mountains.

When the complex scientific explanations for the rise of the Himalayas are considered, the simple poetic myths of the natives take on a new significance. They are easy to comprehend and few people take them seriously while modern geologists have waxed bitter in arguing their views of the mountain-forming process. Some mountains are of volcanic origin where molten magma from beneath the Earth's surface has forced its way up and built single peaks and chains of mountains. There was once a theory that the stupendous forces below the crust could force whole areas upwards as plateaux or mountains if the magma could not break through them. This is less difficult to believe when one realizes that a push of several thousand metres is not great when compared to the size of the Earth. If our planet were shrunk to the size of a billiard ball, eight kilometre (five mile) high Everest would be a hardly discernible pimple upon it. This volcanic theory of the formation of the Earth's ridges and mountains has never explained everything, however, and it has recently been replaced by the theory of plate tectonics. This holds that the Earth's surface is composed of a number of moving plates which raise ridges when they collide and override each other's margins. The exceptional height of Everest can be attributed to the collision of the Indian and Asian plates.

The most startling thing about the Himalayas is that they are such young mountains. The raising of this great ridge has been a fairly gradual process, but much of it has taken place in the last few million years – since mankind has evolved. The very beginnings of mountains in the north of India occurred about 70 million years ago. Before that time India was part of a southern continent embracing South Africa and Australia and it was divided from Asia by the Tibetan sea. The southern continent broke up and India moved slowly north towards Asia. As the thick continental crusts closed inexorably in on one another, the weaker sediment-encrusted floor of the Tibetan sea gave way and was, in effect, crumpled and pushed up on to the northern rim of India to form a mountain chain. Much later – about seven to ten million years ago – the pressure exerted by the collision of the edges of the continents resulted in a further buckling of the edge of India which brought up more uplands. No more than a million years ago the whole Tibetan zone was raised some 3,800 metres (12,500 feet) as the buried layers of lightweight rock 'floated' up to a higher level in balance with the adjacent continent. In a series of final stages the Himalayas were pushed up by the pressure between the two continents. This pressure was so intense that the edges of the rock masses were not just thrust over one another but were also squeezed upwards. At the end of this titanic struggle Everest was the highest place on Earth.

So the birth of mighty Everest involved colossal pressure from the clash of continental land masses. It is extraordinary that these events occurred so recently, and that they may not even be over yet. The lofty Himalayas have been shaken by great earthquakes in recent times, and the mountain-building pressure is still there.

Death Valley

Death Valley is the grim name of a depression that lies at the deepest point on the surface of the western hemisphere. It is 225 kilometres (140 miles) long and between 8 and 24 kilometres (5 and 14 miles) wide – a deep gutter that runs through south-eastern California near the Nevada border. The Valley is a place of extremes: its lowest point is 86 metres (282 feet) below sea-level, and it holds records for intense heat and aridity. Although there is some sparse surface water in parts of the Valley, its average annual rainfall is only 4.22 centimetres (1½ inches) and in some years there is no rain at all. These extremes of climate make it a formidable obstacle to the unprepared explorer and have given it its name. It was christened in 1849 after the fatal journey of a party of emigrants in search of a river in the Valley. It is bounded on the east by the Black and Funeral mountains whose names bear testimony to the sufferings endured by the first parties of Europeans to reach the area, now known as Death Valley.

Such parties of emigrants who pioneered the Wild West were encouraged by government policies which promoted the idea of 'Americanizing' the West. The nation's so-called 'Manifest Destiny' was in part a bid to reduce the Indian and Spanish presence. The settlers, however, were often misled by the contradictory reports about the different trails. John Frémont was one of the first explorers to lead an expedition to California, and later some of his assertions were bitterly challenged by those taking his advice: the Mormon leader, Brigham Young, found to his chagrin that Frémont's 'bucolic' spot near the Great Salt Lake was in fact a bleak and barren desert.

Death Valley may be the hottest place on Earth. A shade temperature of 57° C (134° F) was recorded there in 1913 and this is the highest undisputed shade temperature recorded anywhere. It is remarkable that a place which is not in the tropics and lies on the same latitude as the temperate Rock of Gibraltar (36°) should register such high temperatures. It is, of course, not subjected to the cooling effect of the sea-water which surrounds Gibraltar and, because of its shape, it also tends to cook the thermometer. Heat is reflected from the hard, bare valley sides and from the rocks of its rugged terrain.

It is the depth of Death Valley which makes it so special. It is at the south-western extremity of a region which contains numerous similar but much shallower depressions. A whole area of 1300 by 800 kilometres (800 by 500 miles) east of the Cascade and Sierra Nevada mountain ranges is popularly known as the Great Basin. The whole of the Great Basin suffers from a shortage of rainfall and has no indigenous drainage system apart from the Snake river in the far north. No water drains out of Death Valley itself as evaporation easily accounts for any that finds its way in. In earlier times, perhaps only 2,000 to 5,000 years ago, the Valley harboured a shallow lake. The evaporation of this lake has produced the present salt pan which lies in the lowest part of the Valley.

Although it is a number of features rather than one particular distinction that makes Death Valley so remarkable, it will always be best known for the harsh extremes which its name implies: it is the driest area of North America, one of the hottest places in the world and part of its floor forms the lowest land area in the western hemisphere.

Right: A lone and scrubby bush is the only living thing to be seen in this part of Death Valley.

The Stone Towers of Arizona

Below: The great stone towers of Monument Valley are dramatically picked out when the sun is low in the sky. Their shadows stretch for great distances over the rock-strewn floor of the desert.

Of all the strange sights on Earth the buttes of Monument Valley are the nearest to the fantasy world of dreams. On a high plain in Arizona the wildest assortment of red stone towers and spires stand out starkly and dramatically. Throughout all Arizona the incredible effects of aeons of erosion have produced different and startling forms of what is known as Desert Gothic. This pseudo-architectural title for the works of nature is nowhere more appropriate than Monument Valley in which the vast and

eerie rock formations seem to have a mocking, surrealist resemblance to the castles and cathedrals of medieval Europe. It is a place where the imagination runs riot. By the 'doors' of the great, red rock cathedral stand pillars known as the Three Sisters and one of them, the Prioress, has such an uncannily accurate profile of a cowled figure, with its hands meekly clasped in prayer, that it is hard to remember that this is a 243 metre (800 foot) natural pillar and not the work of a sculptor. The air of the valley is very clear

Left: Some layers of rock are more resistant than others to the wearing effect of wind and rain. A tough top cap is left supported by a more eroded sub-layer on this strangely shaped rock in Arizona's Monument Valley.

and this adds to the sense of unreality as the 305 metre (1,000 foot) high buttes always seem to be much nearer than they actually are. The two Elephant's Feet on the Colorado plateau are the stuff that nightmares are made of – the bases of these colossal sandstone columns have been eroded to resemble the toes of an elephant so much that one half fears, uneasily, to find the rest of a monster lying nearby.

The scenic marvels of the valley are monuments to the landscaping effect of wind and water. Desert is perhaps too harsh a word for the area but it only receives about 20 centimetres (8 inches) of annual precipitation, much of it snow. Many centuries of such a light attack from the elements produce very little erosion and the monoliths of Monument Valley do not change noticeably in the span of a human lifetime. But it is not just centuries or millennia since the rocks of north-east Arizona were laid down but hundreds of millions of years. During these unimaginable stretches of time even the present weather conditions would wreak havoc upon the soft sandstone of the area. There have been enormous changes both in climate and the landscape of North America since the early Mesozoic period which produced this valley's rocks.

During the Permian period 230 million years ago, much of south-west North America was covered by shallow seas. At this time and later, in the Triassic and Jurassic periods, the sand was laid down on the floor of these seas in certain areas, including Monument Valley, and was later compressed to form sandstone. In succeeding ages extensive uplifts of the land occurred and sub-aerial erosion saw the removal of great thicknesses of rock down the stream beds which are now the Colorado and San Juan Rivers. The upper layers of sandstone were harder and more resistant than the underlying shales. So once the caprock sandstone was breached, the lower shale was rapidly eroded. Since then the buttes have been attacked by wind, rain and frost which have further etched them into weathered shapes. In some places canyon walls have been undercut leaving caves and natural bridges as if they were rooms and windows in these strange buildings. Such natural fortification was well exploited by the local Indian tribes, and in the Canyon de Chelly the ruins of ancient adobe homes can still be seen within the caves.

The rugged desert terrain of north Arizona was the homeland of the Navaho Indians. They were a pastoral people, renowned for their skill as horsemen and for the sophisticated and highly inventive weaving of the Navaho women. Their garments and rugs were highly prized by other tribes and exported as far as Mexico. The Navahos suffered removal to a reservation in 1864 after unrest during the Civil War, but the government eventually allowed them to return to their beloved mountains and canyons.

When the evening sun is low in the sky, the shadows of the tall stone towers extend for kilometres over the sagebrush of the valley floor. Some of the rock pillars are monuments indeed – beneath one rock a Navaho Indian lies buried with his horse, and by two others rash prospectors were murdered by Indian bands. These monuments compare with the grandest and most beautiful mausoleums constructed by human beings for they are as massive as the Pyramids and as haunting as the Taj Mahal.

Left: An example of the startling forms, known as 'Desert Gothic', produced by erosion in Arizona. The Canyon de Chelly has been carved out of red sandstone by its river.

The Great Caves and their Decorations

Beneath the ground there is another world. Few people have any conception of the endless kilometres of passages in uncounted subterranean warrens or of the great, fantastically decorated caverns that lie in the unlit depths of the Earth. There are underground rivers, streams and glaciers which flow unseen along limestone channels. They have not attracted much human interest which may in part be due to subconscious fears – a claustrophobic terror of being lost or sealed up in the dark labyrinth, a terror reflected in many works of fiction from *Sinbad the Sailor* to *Tom Sawyer*. Besides this, some caves, especially in the tropics, have an extremely uncongenial atmosphere; their roofs cluttered with gigantic colonies of flea-ridden bats, their floors a heaving mass of cockroaches and stinking droppings, while enormous spiders and blind white fish are among the inhabitants of this special world.

The size and magnificence of some cave systems or individual caverns are stunning. The known length of the Flint-Mammoth system in Kentucky in the United States is over 290 kilometres (180 miles) while the huge Pierre St Martin in the French Pyrenees is so awesomely deep that its lowest level is 1,330 metres (4,369 feet) below its highest entrance. The Big Room in America's Carlsbad Caverns is 91 metres (300 feet) high, twice as wide and 1,220 metres (4,000 feet) long – a colossal chamber, richly decorated with massive stalagmites. The stalagmites of the Big Room are grand enough, but even they do not compare with the exotic and strangely beautiful stalagmites of the picturesquely named Virgin Forest in the Aven Armand pothole in France. Some of the tall, slender, calcite columns of the Virgin Forest stand 30 metres (100 feet) high. This welter of statistics gives only an inkling of the sheer size and extent of the underground world.

Although there are different types of cave, the greatest have all been cut from limestone. The process of underground erosion takes place wherever there is water and either limestone or gypsum as bedrock. Caves or covered corridors of some length can also be formed by volcanic lava as it cools and forms a solid crust while still flowing. There are also beautiful and glittering caves of ice where melt-water has worked on the inside of glaciers after seeping through their crevasses. But the ice caves are ephemeral phenomena due to be destroyed by the movement of the glacier, and lava flows only produce covered corridors – not great caverns or networks of passages. The great cave systems are all to be found in rocks which are soluble in water. Gypsum, which is highly soluble, produces some notable tunnels and caverns but it is a much rarer substance than limestone, so this means that the greatest caves are usually formed in limestone.

The actual process by which water carves great underground systems from limestone is not absolutely straightforward. Water which contains carbon dioxide is able to absorb greater amounts of calcium carbonate (limestone) than water which is unadulterated by carbon dioxide. To a large extent, the creation of limestone caves and their decorations is involved with the amounts of carbon dioxide held and released by rainwater as it sinks into the earth. As rainwater seeps through surface soil it absorbs carbon dioxide which greatly increases its potential for absorbing the lime-

stone into which it then sinks. As it works its way down, each drop of water dissolves a tiny amount of limestone which makes an opening and consequently an easier path for any succeeding drops. As more and more of the surface water finds its way down through already opened fissures these tiny threads widen into channels. This never-ending process of developing the easiest path means that the limestone is not evenly and regularly pierced by water running straight down through it but tends instead to concentrate its water channels so that they become larger and fewer. As time passes some of these channels may combine to form underground stream passages in which the water runs strongly enough to wear at the limestone as well as dissolving it. A combination of gravity and weakness or faults in the rock directs the course of the water as it runs freely and cuts into the rock, or flows slowly and dissolves tunnels through the limestone. Eventually this water action cuts out a great network of caves limited only by the size and composition of the limestone

bed and by the amount of water that runs through it.

There is an immense difference in shape between caverns cut by free-flowing water and tunnels which have been bored through the rock by steady dissolution. This is illustrated by the recognizable similarity of shape between most of the colossal system of dry passages which make up Flint-Mammoth, the longest cave labyrinth in the world. These slightly elliptical tubes were all formed while completely flooded unlike 'vadose' caves in which running water has eventually cut a canyon so that a considerable height can exist between the surface of the stream and the cave roof. In the 'phreatic' passages of Flint-Mammoth the flow-rate of the water was so low that very little abrasion of the cave walls and floor took place. Instead of cutting its way down into the cave floor, the water moved slowly along the flooded caves completely filling them and so eroding the walls, roof and floor equally as it dissolved the limestone. Instead of cutting a canyon the stream

should have dissolved out a cylindrical tube. In fact the Flint–Mammoth tubes are elliptical because the particular bed of limestone which forms the walls of the tubes was of a different texture and thus more easily soluble than the beds of limestone which form the roofs and floors.

Indeed, it is the composition of the limestone that explains the great length and present dryness of the Flint–Mammoth system. Limestone is a sedimentary rock laid down in layers on the beds of ancient seas. Over the ages the face of the globe has changed vastly, and aeons ago great seas have come and gone over the area that is now the state of Kentucky. These seas laid down a very wide bed of limestone where Mammoth Cave Ridge and Flint Ridge are now to be found and over this a layer of porous sandstone was later deposited. Earth movements then uplifted the limestone and eroded away some of the sandstone, so that rainwater could attack the limestone and slowly dissolve the cave system as a form of giant, natural, flooded drain. Eventually the

valley through which the Green River now flows was cut deeper during the harsh climates of the Ice Age and the limestone bed was suddenly left high and dry. The water drained out of the kilometres of underground passages to leave them in their present dry, fossilized state. This means that the water no longer wears steadily away at the cave in its former phreatic manner and so development of the cave system is virtually at a standstill.

The processes which formed Pierre St Martin, the deepest cave in the world, were obviously different from those that formed Flint–Mammoth which is a remarkably level system with very few shafts. Here the limestone was folded by the great alpine earth movements, so that it is steeply inclined and the easiest route for the water has been much more vertical in the Pierre St Martin, less than in the great Kentucky complex where it is almost completely confined to one horizontal bed. The more spectacular rate of erosion in the Pierre St Martin is neatly demonstrated by its greatest chamber. This

Above right: The complex process of calcite deposition in England's Easegill Caverns has drawn slim, elegant straws down from the ceiling and built stumpy stalagmites up from the floor.
Centre right: A magnificent, densely packed display of cave decorations covers the roof of the Grotte de Clamouse in France. Calcite screens, straws and stalactites can be seen amid other dripstone shapes.
Far right: This tangled cluster of helictites has formed in the GB cave in the English Mendips. Helictites grow in any direction depending on the capillary action of water in their hollow centres.

vast, circular room (240 metres in diameter and 130 metres high or 800 feet by 450 feet) is called La Verna and is numbered among the largest cave chambers in the world. The Pierre St Martin is largely a vadose cave, cut out of the rock by the abrasive power of debris carried in its swift-flowing underground river as well as being dissolved by the water. The cave river which has created this deep hole is sizable.

Nearly all the extraordinary and striking decorations for which caves are famous are only able to form in a vadose cave. Stalagmites and stalactites are only two of the many beautiful decorations that can be found underground. There are the fragile straw stalactites, columns made where stalagmites and stalactites fuse, curtains of calcite formed like a hanging sheet where water trickles down a sloping cave ceiling, the descriptively named cave popcorn and many other eerie formations. Some caves are almost bare while others have such a luxuriance of decoration that it is the dripstone which is their chief and overwhelming attraction.

The Aven Armand pothole in France is remarkable enough, but its most famous feature is undoubtedly the grove of fabulously tall and uniquely shaped stalagmites, known as the Virgin Forest. Each of these slender, unusually coloured stalagmites is constructed like an enormous pile of tumblers stacked one within another. Although

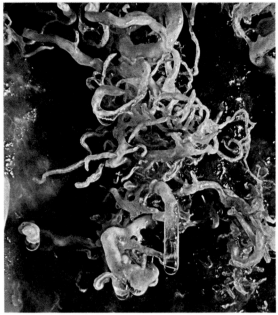

there are similarities of type between cave decorations, no two cave interiors are the same. Among the enormously varied underground world of the beautiful and the grotesque there are plenty of striking or dramatic examples of dripstone shapes, but the Virgin Forest provides an unrivalled spectacle and is one of the best known.

The size and appearance of cave decorations depend upon a number of factors which are unique to each cave. Once again it is the presence of carbon dioxide in water which determines the action the water takes upon the limestone. Rainwater, which is rich in carbon dioxide, is able to dissolve and hold more limestone as it oozes down through tiny fissures in the rock than it would manage if it were free of carbon dioxide. When a drop of this water reaches the roof of a cave or passage it hangs there charged with its extra large load of dissolved limestone. But the air in caves is normally very short of carbon dioxide so the gas in the drop of water begins to diffuse out of it and into the cave's atmosphere. Without the carbon dioxide the water is no longer chemically capable of holding so rich a solution of calcium carbonate (limestone) and so it deposits a drop of this on the ceiling as the mineral calcite (crystalline calcium carbonate). The drop of water is eventually pushed off its perch by the next drop and, when it lands on the cave floor, it deposits some of its remaining calcium carbonate as it joins some underground stream.

Over some time this continued dripping into caverns can build up very considerable quantities of calcite either on the ceiling or the floor or both. The calcite can take many strange shapes, but the most common are the stalactites which hang from the ceiling and the stalagmites which are built up from the floor. The size and shape of these depend upon the type of limestone, the rate of water-flow and the composition of air in the cave chamber. If a drop of water is very

quickly pushed off the ceiling by its successor, it does not have time to deposit much calcite there but retains a lot to leave on the floor. This means a more rapid growth of stalagmite than of stalactite – although the stalagmite will not be very slender. Slender stalagmites are created when the drops that fall on their heads have very little calcite left in them and what remains is instantly deposited, whereas water that is very rich in calcite deposits some on the top of the stalagmite and some down its sides as it runs

Below: A human figure illustrates the colossal size of the main gallery of the Pierre St Martin cave in the French Pyrenees. This great chamber is part of the deepest cave system in the world.

Right: The fabulous stalagmites of the Virgin Forest in France's Aven Armand cave. These slender and delicate stalagmites include the tallest in the world. Regular changes in the rate of drip within the cave have produced a remarkable stacked-tumbler effect which gives these stone decorations a resemblance to the trunks of palm trees and earns them their sobriquet of 'Virgin Forest'.

away – a process which develops a more conical shape.

The strange and lovely symmetry of the 'trees' in the Virgin Forest owes something to other factors. There may be a regular change in the drip rate in the Aven Armand cavern, but what causes this change or whether it is merely seasonal is not known. The immense 32 metre (100 foot) height of some of the stalagmites in the Aven Armand makes them the world's tallest and they are certainly unrivalled in length by stalactites because the tensile strength of calcite is not sufficient to support such monsters.

Dramatic though it is, the Virgin Forest is only one example of cave decoration.

Every cave is different in size and shape and they contain an unbelievable variety of dripstone formations. The repellent bat and cockroach infested caverns of the tropics do not tell the whole story. There are silent dry caves where the waters have been drained away to lower levels. There are wet caves which resound to the roar of fast-moving water and some contain spectacular waterfalls as well as streams and rivers. Some caves may have shelving floors covered in stalagmites or encrusted with bat droppings while others have flat, dry floors where vanished streams have left a layer of sand and silt. The underground world is endlessly varied and full of visual excitement.

The Sahara Desert

Embracing nearly nine million square kilometres (three million square miles) the Sahara is the largest desert on Earth. This enormous tract of barren land possesses almost every variety of desert terrain. Not only are there vast seas of moving sand dunes which are usually associated with desert, but stone plateaux and arid wildernesses of rock pillars as well. There is no entirely satisfactory definition of the sort of conditions that constitute a desert because botanists, geologists and zoologists all have their own ideas on the subject.

If we take a desert to be an arid area which is hostile to most forms of life, the Sahara is very definitely just such an area and, moreover, one that seems to be winning in the hostilities. Aridity can be generally defined as 25 centimetres (10 inches) or less, of annual rainfall. Land in the middle of a great continental land mass is protected from rainfall both by its distance from the seas, which means that winds have usually dropped their moisture already, and by mountain ranges. Most of the world's deserts, including the Sahara, are clustered around the Tropics of Cancer and Capricorn where the prevailing winds are very dry, having lost their water to the north or south. Within these areas, on the western shores of the continents, the cold ocean currents cool the onshore winds and little rain is deposited on the land.

The vast size of the Sahara also ensures that some of its interior will be unusually dry. Not only is it dry, but the cloudless skies result in very high daytime temperatures of about 43° C (109° F) and very cold nights in which the temperature sometimes drops below freezing point. Dryness, but not the extremes of temperature, be-

come exaggerated as one goes deeper into the desert regions. Kebili on the northern edge of the desert has an annual mean rainfall of 83 millimetres (3.27 inches) while Murzuq in the interior has a mere eight millimetres (0.32 inches). Yet Kebili, where 55° C (131° F) has been recorded, is one of the hottest places in the desert. This is because of the Khamsin or Sirocco, a burning south wind which feels like a blast from an open oven and pushes the hot air of the central desert towards the north.

The geology of the Sahara is comparatively simple. It is a very old rock shield dating from the Pre-Cambrian age – one of the earliest in the Earth's history. In those times the area contained massive mountain ranges which were eroded in subsequent ages into a vast, bare platform. Even today half of the Sahara consists of great level plains and depressions of this ancient rock. Later, the area was repeatedly immersed under the sea so that layers of sedimentary rock were deposited in places. Succeeding ages produced a certain amount of volcanic activity and the Sahara's highest surviving volcano, the Tahat, is 2,917 metres (9,570 feet) high. The result of this long geological history is that mountain ranges and isolated volcanic peaks alternate with stony uplands and barren plains in the landscapes of the Sahara.

The most fascinating parts of the desert are its great sand seas which are known in Arabic as *erg*. Most of us who live in less rugged environments visualize all deserts as rolling sand dunes. It is hard to know whether to blame Hollywood and Rudolph Valentino or to hold the late German Field Marshal Rommel and the British 8th Army responsible, but western man has a concept

Above: These hardy date palms grow in southern Morocco and survive in the barely moist soil of a wadi.
Right: The Tassili N'Ajjer mountains of southern Algeria are an ancient and heavily eroded chain. Sparse vegetation can be seen in the valley of this harsh landscape.

Above: The sand dunes of this erg in the Algerian Sahara resemble immobile ocean rollers. They have been formed by the action of the wind and their surfaces are covered with tiny ripples.

of the desert as a sand sea. In huge areas of the Sahara this concept holds good. In the more humid periods of the world's history great rivers wore into the Sahara rock and left the fine debris in hollows. The wind turned these deposits into sand and their dunes smother great areas varying from 38,000 to 100,000 square kilometres (15,000 to 39,000 square miles). The Chech Erg, the Great Western Erg, the Great Eastern Erg and the Ergs of the Sudan, the Tibesti, the Libyan desert and the Tenere and Bilma represent a great deal of authentic sandy desert. The

dunes of some areas are constantly on the move and are advancing in one place at 11 metres (36 feet) a year before the wind and threatening the great oasis of Faja. In other places the dunes are so stationary that there is evidence that the troughs between them have been used as thoroughfares since Stone Age times, although nowadays camel caravans are rapidly becoming a thing of the past as trade goods are increasingly carried by truck.

The famous oases of the Sahara are another puzzling aspect of its character. It seems

absurd that small cultivated islands should survive in the aridity of the great, barren waste. However, a considerable amount of ground-water exists in deeply buried permeable rocks and the water-table may be very close to the surface in places such as the Souf area, or it may at least be near enough for deep wells to be sunk to it. The most important oasis crop is the date palm, in whose shade grow citrus fruits and other less hardy vegetables such as olives, figs and sweet potatoes. There is evidence, however, that even the primitive agriculture of the desert peoples is proving too much for the available supply of ground-water and the water-table is slowly sinking. The only immediate source of replenishment for this dwindling asset is the meagre winter rain which is allowed to soak into the porous soil.

The Sahara is never likely to be anything but barren until the problem of its aridity is solved. That is to say that until some cheap, easy and supremely efficient method of desalinating sea-water is devised, the whole of this vast region will retain its present essential character.

The Barringer Meteorite Crater

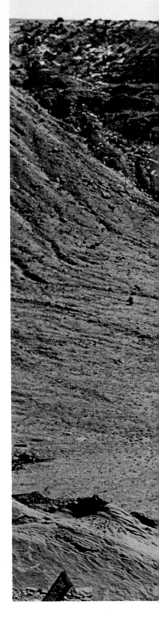

On a level plain in Arizona near Canyon Diablo there is a gigantic crater. The hole is 177 metres (580 feet) deep and 1,250 metres (4,100 feet) across – a strange scar on an otherwise flat surface. This was the first place in the world to be suspected of being a meteorite crater. The heaped up rim around its five kilometre (three mile) circumference and its regular shape bear an uncanny resemblance to the smaller scale features of conventional shell-holes or bomb craters. In fact the projectile which blasted the Barringer crater out of the Arizona sandstone was an estimated two million tonnes of extra-terrestrial material which came hurtling down on to the Earth from the vast, empty spaces of the universe. The crater was discovered in 1891.

It is still a matter of dispute that the Barringer crater was caused by a meteorite, but the weight of scientific proof leaves little room for such speculation. After many years of debate, there is still not absolute agreement on the origin of craters on the moon. It is widely accepted that they are of meteoritic origin, but some vulcanologists still believe that a number of them are volcanic. Suspected meteorite craters on Earth can be as large as the Vredefort Ring in South Africa with its 41 kilometre (26 mile) diameter, but the Barringer is the largest in which meteoritic material has been found to corroborate mere theory. The Barringer has not only the necessary geological features to distinguish it from a volcanic crater or sinkhole, but also the high pressure form of coesite (not previously known as a mineral) has been found in the crushed sandstone of its bottom – conclusive proof of a violent impact.

It was, at first, a problem to explain why the meteorite at the Barringer crater had disappeared. The origin of meteorites is still the subject of dispute. The only thing that may safely be said about them is that they are chunks of extra-terrestrial matter which cross the Earth's path and occasionally crash into it. The Barringer crater had obviously been caused by a huge piece of matter, and it was therefore disturbing to find that most of it had disappeared.

The truth is that the meteorite which blasted down at Canyon Diablo was so big that it was blown to bits by the impact. A fully loaded 40-tonne truck thundering along the motorway at a steady 100 kilometres (60 miles) per hour takes much bigger brakes and a lot more stopping than a quarter-tonne family saloon moving at the same speed. In the same way, the bigger the meteorite the more stopping it takes. Meteorites are not stationary in space but hurtle along on their own orbits and, when they are on a collision course with planet Earth, they feel the first touch of the brakes when they hit the atmosphere. Space is, as its name implies, nearly empty of matter, but the Earth's atmosphere presents an increasingly dense array of particles of gas and dust to any intruder from space. Gas or air may seem like feeble opposition to us but it provides enough friction to have a very marked slowing effect on small meteorites. Indeed, all meteorites of up to approximately one tonne in weight are brought to a halt by the atmosphere which means that they completely lose their cosmic velocity (the speed at which they were travelling through space). Once the projectile is halted, gravity takes over and it falls to the ground.

But the atmosphere does not stop the bigger meteorites. The heavier the projectile

Above: The crater left by the Barringer meteorite in Arizona. Little of the meteorite was found there because it exploded when it reached the ground. Minerals, formed under high pressure, have been discovered in the crushed sandstone of the crater floor.

the bigger the crash when it reaches the Earth's surface. Meteorites of one tonne and more have a cosmic velocity of at least ten kilometres (six miles) per second when they reach the atmosphere and the bigger ones retain more speed than the smaller ones The energy of the moving meteorite is totally expended in friction and turned into heat. The sudden full stop as it hits the Earth produces an instant outpouring of heat as the energy is released.

But the bigger the meteorite the more energy it holds and the more stopping it takes. Meteorites of 100 tonnes and more are hardly slowed up by the atmosphere and are hurtling along with tremendous energy when they are stopped dead by their impact with the ground. The heat given off by this final, brutal braking of a really big meteorite is enough to vaporize it in an explosion. This explains why no meteorite greater than 100 tonnes has ever been found. It also explains why the Barringer crater is empty because an estimated three million tonnes of debris from the Barringer meteorite has been located. This would make a sphere of 152 metres (500 feet) in diameter and when that landed there must have been a tremendous explosion.

So the scar on Arizona's surface was made by the cosmic equivalent of a bomb. The vast, eerie crater is enormously spectacular because it stands in a level plain, uncluttered by rival features. It is, however, without any natural beauty and charm as it looks to be just what it is – a rude imposition on the Earth's surface made by a colossal chunk of extra-terrestrial matter.

The Mississippi Delta

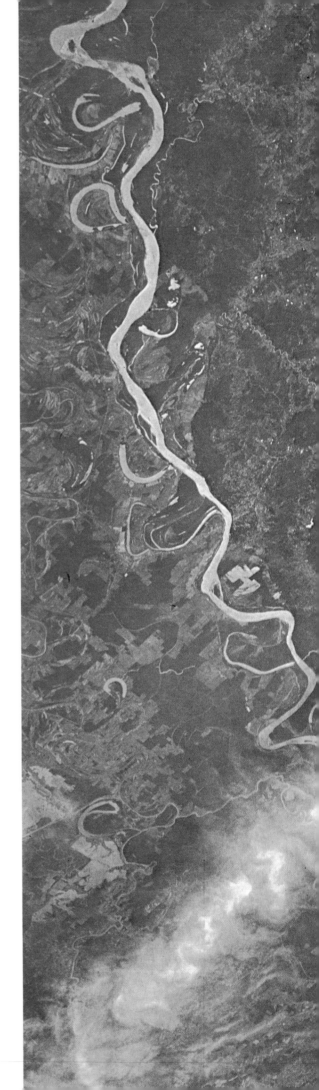

Right: This aerial view of the lower reaches of the Mississippi was transmitted from the NASA Apollo 9 space capsule. It illustrates perfectly 'Old Muddy's' meandering course.

Covering 46,620 square kilometres (18,000 square miles) the Mississippi river delta, opening out into the Gulf of Mexico, is the largest single delta in the world. There is more delta land where the spoil from the Indian rivers Ganges and Brahmaputra meets, but the Mississippi delta issues the largest volume of silt from the mouth of one river. This is not surprising when one realizes that 'Old Muddy' carries one million tonnes of sediment out into the Gulf of Mexico every day of the year – enough to make a block of land 2.5 square kilometres (one square mile) in area and 91 metres (300 feet) high. So far this torrent of silt, sand and mud has built a delta region which stretches 273 kilometres (170 miles) along the coast and 177 kilometres (110 miles) deep from the inland hills to the open sea. The Mississippi crosses the region diagonally from upstream of Baton Rouge where the first of its great distributaries, the Atchafalaya, leaves on its right bank. Midway along its course lies New Orleans, but it is still another 160 kilometres (100 miles) down the river's main channels from that famous city to the open sea.

The building of the delta followed the course of a long struggle between the Mississippi and the ocean currents. The river is one of the chief agents of the endless process of erosion which, over long periods of time, wears all land flat until new mountain-forming processes take place in movements of the Earth's crust. The spoil which is washed into the river over its whole gigantic drainage area of 3,220,000 square kilometres (1,244,000 square miles) – about six times the size of France – is carried by the force of its current out to sea. Most of this sediment comes from the easily eroded soil

through which its right bank tributaries
pass: soil like that of the Bad Lands of
Dakota. When all this silt reaches the sea it
finds a comparatively gently shelving shore,
slight tides and only very mild currents due
to a sheltered position in the Gulf of Mexico.
If circumstances were different, offering a
sudden drop into a stiff current backed by
big tides, the silt would be swept away but,
as it is, the Mississippi finds an ideal environment for delta construction. It banks its
sediment up to form new land projecting
into the sea.

The river waters tend to flow in a few
main channels along the lines of least resistance. At present there are five channels
leading out to the sea. They are known
locally as passes and they all start from points
well downstream of New Orleans. The
river's sediment is carried down these passes
and deposited immediately in front of them
and on their flanks. This gives the delta its
distinctive shape as the channels project out
to sea between thin fingers of new land. The
shallow bays in between these growing
fingers of sand and silt are filled in only by
sediment washed in during times of flood
or through relatively minor disturbances –
so their land is built up much more slowly.
This pattern builds a certain instability into
the river's course because, by breaking
through the narrow banks of its channels, it
can find a much shorter and more direct
route to the sea. Over hundreds of thousands
of years it has periodically done this and
changed course. The result is a complex
region of old and new channels, fossil levees
and isolated or semi-isolated stretches of
shallow water – including the great Lake
Ponchartrain, now cut off north of New
Orleans. Elsewhere the areas between the

45

channels include great swamps, bayous and marshlands.

Because the delta is so much an area of marshes and bayous – a bayou is the Deep Southern term for the various natural lakes, canals and sloughs left by the river's changes of course – one would think that its soil would be extremely treacherous and soft. The soil of Mississippi, however, is probably as hard and compacted as soil anywhere else in the world. The volume of silt washed down in the last 11,000 years alone would appear to be sufficient to have constructed a much larger delta and the river has been dropping its sediment in the area for millions rather than thousands of years. One of the reasons why the delta is not much larger is that the weight of constantly deposited new soil has compressed the lower layers to transform them into quite strong materials. As this takes place the sediments compact as the water is squeezed out of them, so the region subsides and more sediment is deposited to bring it back up to sea-level. This compaction of the sediment has produced some strange results: the lush waterways of the delta are sprinkled with occasional islands and domes of solid rock salt or pure sulphur interspersed with gushes of oil. These bizarre mineral outcrops have been squeezed up out of the rocks by the crushing weight of sediment pressing down on them. Such enormous pressure deforms the more plastic rocks – such as salt – and pinches them up towards the surface.

The colossal weight of the constantly growing delta has also produced crustal sag. The solid rocks of the Earth's crust have actually been buckled downwards under the thrust of the mass of sediment. This slight downward expansion of the delta is another

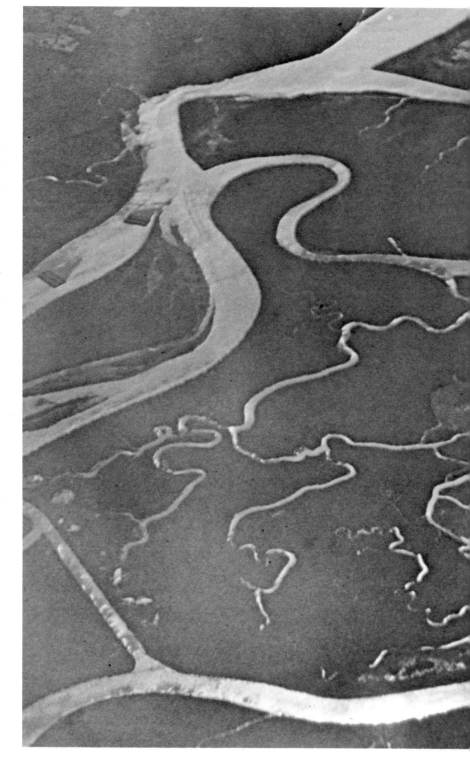

reason why it is not much larger. In effect the huge tonnage of sediment brought down by the river is packed efficiently into a small area which can even expand invisibly downwards. This explains why some of the delta villages, abandoned in historic times, are now drowned in this strange, ever-sinking region and are waiting to be buried by the never-ending flow of silt from the

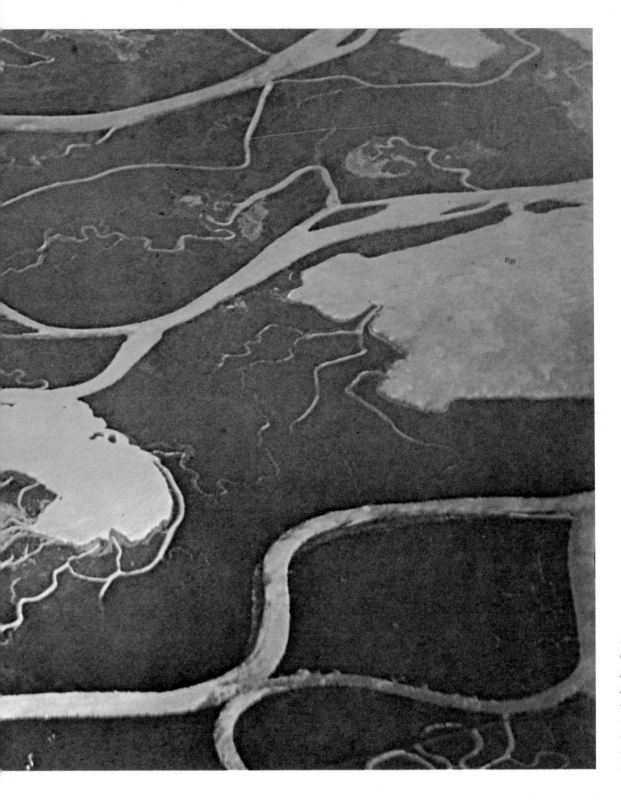

Left: 'Too thick to drink and too thin to plough' – this aerial photograph of the silt-laden waters of the Mississippi shows them splitting into a maze of sloughs and meanders as they reach the delta.

massive reaches of the Mississippi.

It is chiefly around the edges of the delta that the sea has begun to flood back. The weight from the centre of the delta has buckled surrounding rocks and so the area is fringed by huge patches of marshland typified by bayous, cheniers (beach ridges) and natural levees. On the edges of the bayous is the fascinating domain of swamp forest with its aquatic fauna of reptiles and amphibians. The higher and drier part of the delta lies inland – a fertile area of waving grassland. The delta as a whole makes up a unique and complete natural region. To the geologist and the naturalist it is very much an individual place with easily definable boundaries and an interesting character of its own.

47

The Great Rift

The Great Rift is a series of massive trenches 6,000 kilometres (3,700 miles) long. This fault extends through 50 degrees of latitude or one-seventh of the circumference of the globe. The Great Rift is not, strictly speaking, one long single feature but an extensive system of faults and rifts that extends from Mozambique up through Africa, along part of the Red Sea and the Gulf of Aqaba to the Dead Sea and the Jordan Valley. This series of geological cracks has been recognized as a unified system since 1893 when it was given the name of the Great Rift. Along its course it contains a number of deep and imposing valleys which share relatively flat floors and clearly marked sides. Somewhat similar features exist elsewhere in the world, most notably the famous Rhine Graben of Germany and the Baikal Rift Valley of central Siberia. The African-Middle East rifts are occupied by considerable volcanoes, salt flats and over 20 lakes, and they comprise one of the most conspicuous features on the Earth's surface.

The most obvious distinction between the Rift and ordinary valleys is the lack of rivers in the Rift and the scarcity of major breaks in its sides. Also, in common with the Rhine Graben, the Great Rift is not simply a depression but a depression between two raised plateaux. Other great gashes in the Earth's surface, such as the Grand Canyon, are eroded by rivers or glaciers but the virtual absence of eroding rivers in the rifts shows that their origins are tectonic, that is they are attributable to earth movements. The walls of the great trench can tower as much as 2,500 metres (8,200 feet) above its floor although this impressive and sharp contrast does not extend the whole way down all the valleys. The width of the Rift valleys in East Africa, however, is remarkably constant – between 40 and 55 kilometres (25 and 34 miles) and never less than 30 kilometres (18 miles) or greater than 75 kilometres (47 miles).

These figures give only a slight idea of a physical feature which is on so large and impressive a scale that it has determined the boundaries of some modern African states. The Great Rift is a fearsome obstacle which has been of much military importance from the earliest times. It is not accidental that Ethiopia, protectively moated by rift features, was the only African country to escape totally from European expansion during the 'scramble for Africa' in the latter half of the nineteenth century. Today the long lines and arcs of rifts have been responsible for defining the borders of Malawi, Zambia, Tanzania, Zaire, Rwanda, Burundi and Uganda which all have the long narrow lakes of the rift floor or the mountain ranges of the rift walls to form at least a part of their boundaries.

The process which causes rift valleys is not fully understood but there is general agreement that the theory of plate tectonics goes some way towards explaining it. This theory holds that the Earth's surface is composed of a number of vast plates which are constantly, but very slowly, moving. Where these plates collide, one overrides the other, forcing its rock crust downwards and destroying it. Where the plates are tearing apart, effusive, basaltic lava wells up to form new crust. The points at which the various plates are moving apart are mostly beneath the oceans which means that thinner oceanic crust is involved. If the Great Rift is part of this process, however, it falls where two plates are tearing apart along thicker continental crust.

If this is so, the long saga of the drifting continents is being continued as the eastern fringe of Africa stays with Asia, while the rest of Africa drifts gently westwards. This diverging force has caused tears in the rocks in these continents and the central blocks in the rift valleys have slipped down between the inclined faults.

There is not universal agreement, however, that the Great Rift represents a tectonic plate boundary. There are good grounds for questioning the idea that rift valleys are the sites of future ocean basins. The lavas produced on the spreading ocean ridges which mark the boundaries between diverging plates are of a type known as tholeiite. As far as the present day continents are concerned, tholeiitic basalts are only found on their edges. A reconstruction of the immensely long process of continental drift shows that the southern continents of Africa, South America, Antarctica and Australia were all united as one vast continent aeons ago in early Mesozoic times (more than 1,000 million years ago). This supercontinent broke up and its disruption was begun by spreading ridges beneath the continents. Tholeiitic volcanism broke out on the margins of the future continents before actual disruption of the great single continent took place.

The composition of lava is very important as it can tell geologists from what part of the Earth's crust the lava originated and give information on the heat-flow and pressures required to produce it. The problem with the Great Rift is that lavas found within it are non-tholeiitic and are indeed highly variable. Because of this and because of what is known of the origins of rift valley lavas in Kenya and Ethiopia it seems safest to regard

rift valleys as zones of earlier unsuccessful 'attempts' at ocean opening.

The Great Rift provides many dramatic views and varied and exciting natural phenomena from great lava fields to majestic mountains. To the geologist it is an intriguing and mighty fault which is still shrouded in mystery.

Above: A view of the Kenyan Great Rift. It is sobering to think that such a seemingly solid landscape could be undergoing constant change as the Rift widens.

Ayers Rock

At the heart of Australia stands Ayers Rock, beautiful in its remote symmetry. A rounded and almost perfectly regular dome of sandstone, it broods in isolated glory, rising straight from a flat plain which is near the geographical centre of the great southern continent. The rock is red and its profile against the setting sun in this sun-baked land makes it one of the most celebrated sights in the world. One huge monolith nine kilometres (six miles) in circumference and 867 metres (2,845 feet) above sea-level, it bursts abruptly from the scrubby mulga – Australian acacias – of the plain to reach up 335 metres (1,100 feet) in severe loneliness. It is in an area of wide horizons, for from its peak the dry, transparent air gives a view for 96 kilometres (60 miles) over the dreary vastness of level ground, while heights as far as 160 kilometres (100 miles) away can be seen. This clarity of vision tends to draw the prominent features of the place closer together and to understate the great spaces of the interior. Ayers Rock is the most famous and dramatic of three island-mountains which stick out from the flatness of the country south of Alice Springs; 40 kilometres (25 miles) to the west of Ayers is Mount Olga, a rocky outcrop that looks like a clutch of giant eggs, and 80 kilometres (50 miles) to the east is the level-topped table rock of Mount Connor.

Ayers Rock and its companions are rare survivors of the continuous erosion of Australia's ancient rock formations. It is an often quoted irony that one of the youngest nations of the world has the most ancient continent to live on. This does not mean that Australia rose from the sea before any of the other continents but only that its face has remained unchanged by any major earth movements for the longest period of time. In the thousands of millions of years since land first appeared on the surface of the Earth, its contours have been constantly changing. Its history has been basically one of upthrust, during which mountains were built or plateaux emerged from the sea, followed by erosion which gradually levels the mightiest mountains and hardest rocks until they reach (in theory) that ultimate level – so low and flat that the sluggish rivers no longer bear any sediment to the sea. Although Australia is not so reduced, its last mountain-building convulsions were so long ago that it is, in general, a very flat land with no mountain peaks above the permanent snow-line.

In the Proterozoic period starting 2,300 million years ago, the area around Ayers Rock and the plain on which it stands were under a sea that separated the high and mountainous land of Yilgarnia to the south from Stuartiana to the north (geologists

give as unlikely names to the lands of the past as science fiction writers do to potential future worlds). The northern shore of Yilgarnia was fringed by the then mighty Musgrave Mountains. Material worn from the Musgraves was carried into the sea and from it were laid down the rocks of Ayers and similar outcrops in the Cambrian period which began 560 million years ago. Later, when the seas had drained away, the rocks were contorted and folded, so that those of Ayers Rock now stand vertically, and then the area was exposed to the steady, relentless process of erosion. Ayers Rock is a chance residual mass of harder rock. The main agent in lowering the land that surrounds it was water, which was in very much more plentiful supply during certain ages than others.

The long ages of erosion have left their scars upon Ayers Rock itself. From a distance it seems to be a steep but regular dome with precipitous lower slopes and gentler upper slopes rising to a rounded summit. But a closer look shows that its sides are scored with deeply etched gutters. These furrows have been ploughed by countless rainstorms which have worn channels in the weakest rock. Nowadays the annual rainfall is about 12 centimetres (five inches) but rains can fail for years. When Ayers Rock is caught in a cloudburst the gutters down its steep sides become spectacular waterfalls. The ends of these gutters are shaded by the steep sides of the rock and, despite the desert climate, are filled with luxuriant vegetation. In three places there are permanent pools of clear water – a rare and delightful sight in the centre of this harsh continent. In places where the elements have found some weakness the rock has been worn to give shallow caves or shelters and some of these have been decorated by the aboriginal people of Australia. To them the rock is a place of awe 'where the wind moans always between sunset and dawn'.

Above: Ayers Rock has a dramatic silhouette. The cracks and gutters which run down its steep sides can stream with water during a rare cloudburst.

The Petrified Forest

In Arizona lie the remains of a forest in which the trees are of solid stone. The work of some strange, natural logger can be seen in the Chinle Beds. Lying in neat sections are faithful reproductions of trees long dead in glassy silica. The colours of these 'logs' are sometimes a little unusual, but their detail is perfect. One can see roots, parts of slender branches, bark, growth rings and even the cracks and chips which the original trees sustained in life. Similar stone trees have been found in different parts of the world, but they are sometimes cruder copies compared with those in the Chinle Beds and they are certainly never as spectacular or on so large a scale.

The trees are, in fact, fossils: that is to say they are a preserved vegetable organism – although the remains of animals can be fossilized in the same way. Fossils are extraordinarily common and have been preserved by a number of different processes. Sometimes living things are suddenly overwhelmed by a preservative; this is the case of flies caught in amber, the resin of an ancient conifer, which engulfs them and then hardens. All the Earth's vast reserves of coal are the fossilized remains of vegetation which has been through the process of carbonization. On rare occasions living things may become encrusted with minerals – as a leaf might if it dangled in a chalky stream.

The trees of the Petrified Forest are the result of the more common process of mineralization. The turning of the trees into chalcedony and quartz began when they were permeated by a mineral in the sediment in which they were lying – in this case the chalcedonies which were deposited on them. Sometimes the minerals merely fill the spaces between the skeletal elements and produce a crude copy, but the stone trees have undergone a more thorough transformation. Molecule by molecule the silica has replaced the cellulose of the wood and made an exact and faithful image of the original. The parts of a tree, from its rings to its bark, contain varying amounts of different trace minerals such as iron or sulphur, and these have stained the silica in contrast-

Right: This view of jumbled logs from the Petrified Forest shows how the stone fossils have imitated their wooden models in every intricate detail. Differences in colour distinguish the bark from the wood of the tree and old scars can be clearly seen.

A fairly unremarkable set of circumstances has led to the creation of the silica woods in the Chinle Beds. The trees were conifers related to an ancient group called the Araucarians, which are now only found in the southern hemisphere. There was a theory that these trees were washed into shallow lakes by streams and rivers in the Eocene period, but as they, or their fossils, are in such an undamaged state and as many stand vertical, in a position of growth, it is more likely that they grew on the spot. At various times they must have blown over in high winds and landed on the bottom of the lakes where they accumulated to produce the Chinle Beds two hundred million years ago during the Triassic period. The silt at the bottom of these lakes was, in places, 91 metres (300 feet) thick and the trees were held in its clinging embrace while they underwent their metamorphosis into stone. All the rock strata above the silt has since been eroded away and today the silt itself is being worn down by wind and rain so that the hard mineral logs gradually emerge. The original trees have been broken into neat, transverse sections or logs because the stone was hard but brittle; over the ages earth tremors of various intensities have caused the trees to snap as though they had passed through a sawmill.

It seems to be a wonder from a fairy tale – a forest made from precious stones. In fact, chalcedony is only a precious stone in its rarer forms such as agate or opal, and although the quartz can have exotic names such as carnelian or bloodstone, it has no intrinsic worth. So the forest may not be made from valuable gems but it is strange enough and beautiful enough to rival any fairy tale.

ing shades and colours. As a result, not only the shape of the tree has been recreated but also its diversity. The bark of these quartz fossils is dark red–brown and their insides a mauvish grey while roots can be bright yellow. Splits or chips in the 'wood' can be represented by a veritable kaleidoscope of colour and the variety of this jewellery is endless.

THE
PLANT
KINGDOM

There is not much of the Earth's surface which has not been conquered by the all-pervading members of the plant kingdom. Freshwater lakes and salt-water seas are alive with algae and weed; huge evergreen forests survive in the less temperate zones while vast areas of broad-leafed rain-forest cloak the equatorial regions; savannas, prairies and steppes provide rolling miles of grassland while, even in Arctic tundra and desert wastes, lichen and cacti endure the grim conditions, and long-dormant seeds wait for the brief spell of warmth or moisture that enables them to spring to life. Plants can never be long denied – weeds sprout through cracks in the city pavement and an untreated swimming pool will soon turn green with minute specks of vegetation. Much of the world is literally landscaped by its vegetation from the tall palms on a tiny Pacific atoll to the tranquil parkland of the English counties and the giant, brooding cacti of the Sonoran desert. There is a permanence about vegetation that is denied to other forms of life – there are trees still living that were tall when Tutankhamen ruled in Egypt and, even though great forests have been cleared for agriculture, they would soon return if any disaster should strike mankind.

Plants played an early and essential part in the creation of life and they are absolutely necessary to sustain it. It is now believed that before the evolution of living organisms, the Earth had an atmosphere devoid of free oxygen which probably contained only water vapour, methane, ammonia, carbon dioxide and perhaps nitrogen. An atmosphere without free oxygen was ideal for the spontaneous creation of organic molecules – the first step towards producing life-forms. The earliest direct evidence of life is of fossilized blue-green algae three billion years old. Blue-green algae possess a gift unique to the plant kingdom: the ability to photosynthesize – albeit in a modified form. By the process of photosynthesis plants can take and store the energy of sunlight. In doing so they utilize carbon dioxide and water to produce food substances and free oxygen. The oxygen given off by the algae gradually changed the nature of the atmosphere, which is now about 78 per cent nitrogen and 21 per cent oxygen. Since animal life-forms are dependent upon oxygen for their respiration, it can be clearly seen that early plants paved the way for the origins of other forms of life. Even today it is the production of oxygen by plants that maintains the balance against its consumption by respiration and other processes.

All other forms of life are utterly dependent upon plants for energy as well as oxygen. Only plants can photosynthesize and take their energy from the sun so that members of the animal kingdom have to digest plants or other plant-fed animals as an energy source. Plant life is the bottom link in the food chain by which we all exist.

Plants are by no means a humble or inferior form of life. Any account of striking wonders from the plant kingdom should include, of course, plants which give particular evidence of their strength and success such as the magnificent General Sherman tree, but there are also plants which show an unusual ability for purposeful action. Although only the most dramatic examples such as the Venus flytrap appear here, the ability to move is quite widespread throughout the plant kingdom. This movement is

Previous page: Trees in their autumnal glory. They are the most prominent and permanent of plants and nature's crowning embellishment to any landscape.

56

Left: The Trumpet Leaf (Sarracenia flava) *is an elegantly shaped insectivorous plant. Unlike the Venus flytrap it does not rely on movement to trap its victims. A sticky secretion inside the leaf attracts unwary insects which, upon landing, slip down into the base of the trumpet.*

not brought about by the muscles and nerves which members of the animal kingdom possess but by a series of chemicals transmitted through the plant, including hormones and high-energy substances. The mechanisms are more sophisticated than one might expect from humble plants.

There is much which remains to be discovered however, and it is, as always, a most interesting and challenging time for botanists. There is, for example, a continuing need to know why particular plants grow in particular places as the great mangrove stands of the tropics grow in brackish or saline water. A myriad questions remain to be answered: how have the intricate patterns

of the Fly Orchid evolved? Why does the Fairy Ring mushroom grow in a circle? How can the General Sherman tree sustain its great height? Much benefit may be gained from a study of the function and significance of the hundreds of obscure chemicals found in plants (including their possible use in medicine and agriculture). The scientific study of the plant kingdom offers dozens of areas of useful advance. To most of us, plants have only seemed remarkable as a support to other forms of life or when they have been unusual in size, endurance or specialization. Scientific discovery is starting to show that some plant species have previously unimagined capabilities.

The Fairy Ring Champignon

In the early autumn, strange dark rings appear on the grass. They can be seen in meadows and on pasture-land but they seem to occur most frequently on the smooth surface of lawns. The outer edges of these mysterious circles are usually studded with toadstools. These two occurrences, the rings and the toadstools, are obviously connected and oddly perplexing. Toadstools, which are popularly thought to be universally poisonous, have a faintly sinister air as befits fungi feeding off rotten things. The dark, unnaturally lush, green rings are not always permanent but can appear suddenly and surprisingly – often in the same place as a ring appeared the year before. Grazing animals are supposed to shun these rich, rank patches of turf which William Shakespeare described as 'green-sour ringlets'.

Folklore provides a number of unlikely explanations for the rings of toadstools. Some of these explanations are whimsical and charming – some of them are rather less so. Lightning, moles, slugs and snails have been blamed but a number of less innocent and natural agents have also been thought to be the cause. It has been held that these were the tracks of the devil, who was walking round in circles because he was churning his butter during the night. The Germans thought that the rings were marked during the revels of witches who gathered on Walpurgis night for their annual party. The French believed that they were the homes of giant toads with bulging eyes, while the Dutch knew them to be the work of the devil and that they would upset the milk of cows which grazed in them. But the most popular explanation – particularly in Celtic communities from Brittany to Ireland – is that it is the nimble feet of capering fairies which stamp out the mysterious circles as they prance around in some nocturnal frolic.

The dark rings upon the grass, however, are not the work of sprites. They are the tracks of commonplace fungi such as *Marasmius oreades* – the Fairy Ring Champignon. *Marasmius oreades* starts its life growing in a cluster but, as time passes, it pushes out in all directions, becoming an ever-widening ring.

Above: An example of the Fairy Ring Champignon (Marasmius oreades). These mushrooms are the fruiting bodies of fungi which grow outwards from a central point.

This form of life involves the breakdown of the humus and the release of inorganic plant nutrients which benefits the grass and accounts for the lush greenness of the fairy ring. At another stage there is a release of toxins from the fungus, but although this harms the grass causing the rings to go brown it is not because *Marasmius oreades* is living off the grass as a parasite. Where the fungus dies off, its remains will provide nutrition for the grass, another cause for it to turn a greener shade.

Marasmius oreades is not the only ring-forming toadstool or mushroom. Indeed, the terms toadstool and mushroom are misleading as they are not scientific descriptions but those used rather loosely by country folk for various shapes of fungi. Only the cultivated species *Agaricus bisporus*, which makes such an agreeable companion to steak, kidney and oysters, can unambiguously be described as a mushroom although the term is often used for any mushroom-shaped fruiting body. Not all sinister looking toadstools are poisonous – *Marasmius oreades*, for example, is edible. A great deal of discernment and successful identification of fungi is necessary to the aspiring gourmet – particularly as there are almost a dozen separate species of ring-forming fungi.

The real explanation for fairy rings seems rather prosaic beside the fanciful idea that they are resting places for over-extended fairies. It is believed that some of these rings may be very ancient, and that, on rare occasions, the fungus colony which causes them is several hundred years old. If this is true it illustrates a marvel of nature's economy. The dead things on the earth are not wasted but used to sustain a humble form of life which can endure for centuries.

In common with all fungi the Fairy Ring Champignon has no chlorophyll, the green substance which enables plants to trap energy from the sun. Some plants which are devoid of chlorophyll drain living things for their needs and are known as parasites. *Marasmius oreades* gains its energy from humus, dead matter in the grass, and so, because it harms nothing living, is known as a saprophyte.

The General Sherman Tree

The most massive living thing on Earth is the General Sherman tree. This mighty creature is a member of the amazing Sequoia family and its species is officially titled *Sequoiadendron giganteum* to distinguish it from the equally renowned Coast Redwood (*Sequoia sempervirens*). It stands 83 metres (272 feet) tall, but the key to its bulk is its vast girth which is 24 metres (79 feet) when it is measured one and a half metres (five feet) above ground level. The magnificent thing has been estimated to contain 600,120 board feet of timber but sprang thousands of years ago from a pinhead-sized seed. From such humble beginnings it has swelled through the centuries to weigh in at 2,145 tonnes.

The Giant Sequoia is a truly imperial sight. The General Sherman's nearest rival for the title of the world's largest living thing is probably another Giant Sequoia called the General Grant although the Kauri trees of New Zealand are also very large. *Sequoiadendron giganteum* is not a very common creature in its natural habitat. These great and ancient trees grow together in groves on the slopes of the Sierra Nevada mountains in California and occur naturally nowhere else. As a species it remained unknown, save to Indian hunters, until an explorer named John Bidwell stumbled upon a grove in 1841. His reports were disbelieved at first but by 1853 collectors were exporting seeds to the eastern states and to Europe.

The rarity of the Giant Sequoia was quickly appreciated, and so it was saved from the lumber trade and has long been preserved in the national parks of California. In Britain it was named Wellingtonia after the 'Iron Duke' of Wellington who died just before the first seeds reached Europe. This name remains common in Britain.

Seeds of the General Sherman tree have been taken and artificially planted successfully in many places and a lusty, young Giant Sequoia can be seen from my window in the English county of Kent. Only in the Sierra Nevadas are there groves of the really old and mature trees. Counting the rings of large trunks of the species has given an age of at least 3,200 years and it is quite likely that some of those now growing are even older. They are by no means the oldest trees but it is salutary to know that some of the monsters were living and growing while Tutankhamen ruled in Egypt and before Moses led the Exodus.

The oldest trees are not necessarily the largest, however. Almost all mature Giant Sequoias seem to be topped – that is to say that they look to be bald or dead at the top. The reason for this is a matter of conjecture, but it is fair to suppose that it may have something to do with their colossal size or possibly is a result of being struck by lightning. Indeed, if the Giants were not topped it is possible that they would be the tallest as well as the bulkiest trees in the world whereas this title is in fact held by their slimmer cousins, the Redwood trees. This topping of the Giants may be simply a result of the trees' inability to draw up enough moisture to carry on growing.

The process by which water reaches the topmost leaves or needles of a tree has always been a mystery. How can something so small as a leaf draw water up so many metres from the ground? Some of the force required is undoubtedly provided by capillary action. This is the process that makes use of the natural adhesion of water molecules to the

Right: The magnificent General Sherman tree. One of its glories is its thick bark which is immensely soft and springy. It grows among smaller Giant Sequoia trees in a grove in the Sierra Nevada mountains of California.

side of a tube – even a glass of water can be used to demonstrate this strange process. Where the water touches the glass, it can be seen to rise very slightly upwards. If the bottom of a very, very fine tube is placed in water the water molecules will rise right up to the top. The narrower the tube, the higher the water will rise. If the interior of a tree contains numbers of these fine tubes, natural capillary action will provide some upward movement of water. Allied to this is the process encouraged by evaporation of water from the top of the tree. Water molecules have a strong attraction to each other as well as to the sides of a tube so the evaporation of one molecule will pull another into its place and this, in turn, will pull the next molecule along and so on down to the source of moisture. However, this does not fully explain how tonnes of water can be drawn up by the greatest trees and it is apparent that the tree itself employs some of its own energy, in a manner which is still mysterious, to supply its topmost parts.

Despite their topped appearance, the colossal size of the Giants makes them infinitely the most majestic of trees. Standing by their mighty trunks looking up at their blue-green foliage one feels awe at their grandeur and their age. Perhaps their most attractive feature is their soft, enormously thick, red-brown bark. The General Sherman's bark is 61 centimetres (24 inches) thick in places and even the thinner bark of lesser specimens is so soft that a fist can be driven into it without fear of injury.

Among all living things, the Giant Sequoia is the greatest. Planted in the rich, mouldy soil of the Sierra Nevadas, the General Sherman has stood for centuries as the biggest tree on Earth.

Imitative Orchids

The orchid family is an enormous and exotic one, with a staggering range of sizes. There are about 25,000 species of orchids in 700 genera so far discovered and there could be even more to be found in the unexplored parts of the world. In addition to this, there are at least as many cultivated forms and hybrids. Most parts of the world which are not actually hostile to plant life support some species of orchid, from tropical rain-forest to more temperate climes. The family has a mystique of its own and is extremely popular among horticulturists, so that very high prices have been paid for desirable specimens. One of the genus *Cymbidium* was sold in 1952 for U.S. $4,500. Orchids have attracted their admirers because of the beauty and abundance of their flowers, which come in all colours. Although it is a varied family, it is also a highly specialized one and individual species of it use the most bizarre devices to ensure pollination and reproduction.

Some orchids perpetrate astonishingly accurate deceptions. The labellum (lowest petal) of members of the genus *Ophrys* is in the form and colouring of an insect. Whether the orchid is presenting itself as a bee or a fly, the copy is in such tireless and minute detail that only a careful inspection can establish that the image of the insect is, in fact, an extraordinary piece of natural illusion. There are countless examples of camouflage in the animal and plant kingdoms, but the subterfuge practised by the Bee and Fly Orchids is in a completely different league. It is the ambition behind the fraud that is remarkable – it is no petty attempt to hoodwink a cursory glance or to gain protection from a predator, but a replica of photographic accuracy intended to cheat the very insect it represents.

It is for the purposes of reproduction that members of the genus *Ophrys* display their astonishing images of insects and spiders. Orchids, in general, are ingenious and diverse in the contrivances they adopt to ensure pollination. They normally require cross-pollination, which is achieved by a wide range of insects (bees, flies, moths and butterflies) and sometimes by birds. It has been discovered that the Fly Orchid, amongst others, uses its scent to attract insects – giving a very good imitation of the scent the female fly uses to attract the male. At first sight, the illusion produced by the imitating orchids would seem to be a highly sophisticated decoy device, rather like the ploy used by pigeon shooters who place pigeon replicas on the ground to attract real birds. But the idea behind the orchids' display is more complex than this. The Bee Orchid (*Ophrys apifera* and others) is self-pollinating and therefore it does not need to attract insects at all. In fact, the Bee Orchid uses the weighty bumbling of the approaching bee to trigger off the pollinating mechanism in which the pollinia falls over on to the plant's stigma. In certain species of the Fly Orchid, such as *Ophrys speculum*, which do need to be pollinated by another flower, the fly is not attracted to the flower's nectar but by its own image on the labellum. In this case, it is the fly's mating urge, not his feeding urge, to which the appeal is made. *Ophrys speculum* displays an exact replica of the female Campsomeris fly and this image prompts attentive males into performing a courtship dance that brings them into contact with the pollinia.

Such perfect imitation of insects, displayed for such complicated reasons, places strain on the belief that this is the random con-

Left: The Fly Orchid attracts male flies because the lips of its flowers simulate the appearance of the female fly. The deceived male attempts to mate with the 'female' which leaves traces of the orchid's pollen on his body and he then carries the pollen to another similar flower.

clusion of generations of natural selection. The ideas put forward by Charles Darwin in his work *On the Origin of the Species by Means of Natural Selection* apply even to these amazing orchids. This explains that the realistic insect display evolved very slowly and was not instantly created. Darwin demonstrated that there was a 'quiet war' between all species for survival. In this war, the success of certain species is reinforced while the unsuccessful become extinct. According to Darwin's theory, the insect dis-

play would have begun by chance when millions of generations ago the colour pattern on an orchid bore a very crude resemblance to an insect. This crude resemblance was just good enough to give the orchid a better chance of attracting insects and thus of surviving.

No two flowers are absolutely alike and so the descendants of these orchid species vary in minute detail. Every tiny variation which brought them closer to the colour and form of the insect meant a better hope of survival.

Rain over the Desert

Above: Beautiful flowers appear on a cactus in the Colorado desert. Cacti and many other desert plants possess sharp thorns and spikes instead of leaves which would be desiccated in the fierce heat of the sun. The spikes may also afford some protection from grazing animals.

When it rains the desert blooms. Barren tracts of land which nature appears to have abandoned suddenly blaze with colour as long-dormant life awakes. Any region which receives less than 25 centimetres (10 inches) of rain in a year is decidedly arid, and if it receives less than 15 centimetres (6 inches) it can truly be described as desert. In such places the land may appear to be lifeless – a moonscape of rock and sand, hostile to vegetation, so unlike the fertile soils of wetter regions. Yet there certainly is life sleeping in the sand, holding on against the long drought and waiting for replenishment.

When the rain comes at last to the desert the first thing it does, paradoxically, is cause a flood. Anyone who has sat through a centimetre or two of rain delivered continuously will know that this is something more than a shower. The 15 centimetres (6 inches) of rain which desert regions can expect in a year are not evenly spread in time but tend to arrive in sudden cloudbursts. In some deserts rains are seasonal but they can rarely be relied upon so that an absolute drought may last for years. It is quite normal for the rains to make up for this with a deluge.

The desert's surface is especially ill-equipped to cope with a great deal of water. The hard, baked land cannot easily absorb the sudden excess of moisture and so the water tends to run off into old, dry watercourses. The normally dry wadis of the Sahara become foaming torrents and dusty ditches in Australia become first streams, then rivers, while acres of sterile salt flats are buried beneath the sparkling waters of a reborn lake. A complete change comes over the arid landscape and a man can be drowned in a place where a few hours before he could have walked dryshod. These flash floods soon run away into the dust and sand, but while they last they give the desert an unexpected and very different face.

The dry land was never as lifeless as it seemed. In places, desert-hardened species such as mesquite, cacti or euphorbias will be hanging on against the grim conditions ready to take maximum advantage of any rain that falls. Vegetation in the desert is sparse but few areas are totally devoid of it. It is very common for barren tracts of burning waste to be covered with colourful flowers after brief rains. These flowers are from 'ephemeral' plants whose seeds have

been lying in the inhospitable soil until the effect of moisture starts their life-cycle.

The evening primroses which spring up out of the Californian desert after rain are among the most spectacular and well-known of ephemeral plants. Masses of these beautiful, scented plants carpet the desert floor in a short blaze of glory in the spring. This sudden blooming cannot last long, for the usual desert conditions of blazing heat, cold nights and extreme aridity soon overcome the effects of the rain. Because they cannot live long the ephemeral plants push on quickly with their essential life-cycle. Within a few weeks they have to germinate, grow, flower,

pollinate and leave behind seed for a successor to spring up after the next rains. While they are busy, other species of plant – those that are drought-resistant – are also breeding and growing before the next drought forces them to cut back.

Although rainfall is a rare and unreliable phenomenon in desert regions, it is expected, indeed eagerly awaited, by living things which survive through the long droughts. Seeds and plants which have miraculously endured through harsh times make the most of the change. This is what causes the sensational and unlikely spectacle of the desert covered by colourful blooms.

The Venus Flytrap

The Venus flytrap (*Dionaea muscipula*) behaves in an extraordinary manner for a plant. Of all the insect-eating plants, the Venus flytrap is probably the best known and most spectacular. While other insectivores rely on passively holding their prey with sticky secretions or drowning it when it falls into the plant's cups, the flytrap actually closes its hinged leaves shut about the ears of its victims. While its leaves are spread in waiting, the flytrap attempts to give an impression of being an innocent vegetable, but the spiky bristles around its leaves give a clue to its menacing nature. When the signal comes these bristles will interlock holding the leaf closed and entombing its prisoner. This strange, sinister herbaceous plant was described by the eighteenth-century Swedish botanist Carl Linnaeus, who devised today's system of botanical classification, as '*miraculum naturae*' because of its astonishing abilities.

The most surprising thing about the flytrap is its ability to move swiftly to trap its prey. Rapid movement in response to a stimulus is normally confined to the animal kingdom, but is also found in a few plants. The secret of the flytrap's trigger mechanism is three long, stiff hairs which can be seen on each leaf half. An insect which is attracted by the shiny leaves and alights on them is almost certain to knock these hairs. The harder the hairs are hit the faster the leaf will close. These hairs are attached to a mobile pad at the centre or 'hinge' of the leaf and when they are stimulated the cells of the pad contract causing the leaf to fold. Obviously the trigger will occasionally be touched off by indigestible wind-blown flotsam or an unsympathetic human forefinger and then the leaf will close in 15 to 30 seconds on a false errand. A dead object, however, will be left untouched as it will not touch the hairs in succession, the essential trigger for the toothed edges to mesh. If the plant finds that it has caught something which does not have the nitrogen-rich body it craves, the leaf reopens within a day or two.

After the capture, the flytrap squeezes its prey against its digestive glands. These

Right: The leaves of a Venus flytrap at various states of readiness to receive a new victim. Some are wide open while others are less so. The spiky edges of closed leaves interlock to hold their prey fast.

extraordinary behaviour exist in the plant kingdom. *Mimosa pudica,* for example, is another remarkably sensitive plant which reacts to any contact by immediately curling up its leaflets into a tight defensive position. The Mimosa's recovery to its former shape can take several hours. The unusual Sarraceniaceae family contains plants which, like the Venus flytrap, trap insects – only they do so more passively, relying on a slippery viscous fluid.

Most plants, however, do not behave in these peculiar science-fiction ways and certainly the Venus flytrap's carnivorous greed is not typical – trapping and devouring insects is, of course, not a normal activity of plants. Plants usually obtain their food and energy from the sun by the process of photosynthesis. The leaves draw in carbon dioxide from the atmosphere and fix it into carbon compounds which can be drawn on as an energy source. Plants are able to do this because they contain the green substance, chlorophyll. The whole process of photosynthesis is the exclusive property of the vegetable kingdom – animals cannot draw their energy directly from the sun's rays. The Venus flytrap makes the best of both worlds because it not only takes energy from the insects it traps but also from photosynthesis. Flytraps will remain quite healthy if denied insects, but they only become really vigorous when they are trapping and digesting their victims. Flytraps which are kept in captivity should be fed on raw meat or boiled egg. Their lethal habits and craving for protein probably occur because their natural habitat is the nitrogen-deficient bogs of North Carolina and the bodies of ensnared insects make up this deficiency and allow the flytrap to flourish.

glands secrete a viscous mixture, rich in protein-digesting enzymes, which breaks down the victim's corpse. The plant absorbs the dissolved parts of the insect through special cells and slowly opens (after 10 to 35 days) when the chitinous husk of the insect can be seen. Sooner or later it is dried out by the sun and air, and eventually blown away leaving the leaf clean and ready for the plant's next 'meal'. Other examples of

Mangrove Swamps

Vast expanses in the hotter, more humid parts of the world are covered in mangrove swamp. These immense, sombre stretches of gnarled, unexciting looking trees exist in those places which are neither dry land nor entirely under water. The mangrove lives on the banks and flood plains of rivers and also, remarkably, on the salty margins of lagoons and estuaries. The mangroves comprise many different species from several unrelated plant families and thrive in areas which hold particular hazards for vegetation. Some mangrove species are salt-tolerant and can exist in coastal areas far from fresh water: this gives the plants an enormous competitive advantage, as relatively few plants are halophytic (salt-tolerant). Because of these special properties, huge tracts of land in Africa, Madagascar, Indo-Malaysia and the Americas have become mangrove swamp.

Mangrovia tends to expand under its own momentum. The masses of mangrove roots form a dense thicket which impedes tidal currents and hastens the deposition of mud. In this way the trees stabilize the mudflats and create new land. On swampy seashores the Red Mangrove, *Rhizophora mangle*, is the first to start colonization and, as it builds up a barrier of mudflats, the area on its landward side becomes more suitable for less salt-loving species such as the Black Mangrove (*Avicennia nitida*) and White Mangrove (*Laguncularia racemosa*). In the mangrove swamps of Florida these three species grow in separate belts and their distribution is decided by a mere seven to ten centimetres (three to four inches) difference in land level. This tiny difference is enough to determine whether the water is merely brackish, saline or more salty and each mangrove species

Right: Mangrove trees amid the dense tangle of their roots and the prop roots which extend down from their branches. These roots may have helped to collect the mud and build the bank upon which the trees now stand.

takes up its stand in the environment which suits it best.

The muddy soil of the mangrove swamp would prove fatal to a less specialized plant. Although the mud contains a wealth of organic material it is without oxygen, which is necessary to plant roots. The mangrove overcomes this problem by developing a special breathing mechanism, or respiratory root, which grows upward through the mud and rises above the level of the highest tides. These branch roots, sometimes called pneumatophores, absorb oxygen from the air and enable the rest of the buried root to thrive. The appearance of these respiratory roots, which often grow in dense masses, accounts to some extent for the forbidding and tangled look of a stand of mangroves – which has, nonetheless, proved a congenial habitat for an exotic wildlife.

Similar difficulties attend the regeneration of plants in a mud swamp. Seeds which became buried in the mud would suffocate, so the various mangrove species ensure survival by specialized germination techniques. On most mangroves the seed is germinated before it is detached from the fruit so that it will fall into the mud pre-equipped with a root. This root is often up to 30 centimetres (12 inches) long. The seeds of other species are protected by a thick spongy exterior which enables them to float out on the tide until they are caught up in some obstacle where they find conditions are suitable for germination.

This specialization has made the mangrove a vastly successful form of plant life, flourishing as undisputed tenant of immense areas of the globe. The mangrove is adapted in ingenious ways to an unhelpful environment in which it has few competitors.

THE
REALM
OF ICE

Previous page: This South American fjord is still not completely free of ice. It must have contained a vast glacier during one of the great ice ages and lies at the foot of Mount Italia in Tierra del Fuego National Park.
Below: Snow-capped Mount Fitz Roy shows white over the dreary wastes of Patagonia in Argentina. The rock has been ground into sharp peaks by the pressure of ice.

Great ice sheets still exist in the Arctic and in the Antarctic – where they hold an entire continent in their grip. At the moment these ice sheets are far from cities and centres of population, but the lesson of history is that one day they will begin to advance again. When they will begin to grow and how far they will come is entirely a matter of speculation, but if ice ever re-attains the hold that it had 10,000 years ago much of northern civilization would be imperilled: Scandinavian and Canadian cities would be overwhelmed together with Berlin and Leningrad while London, New York and Chicago would be menaced. The evidence suggests that such a great change in climate would be gradual and that it would hardly be perceptible over the span of a single human generation. On the other hand historic times have shown a number of marked and fairly sudden changes in climate which would be apparent during a lengthy

lifetime. The period from A.D. 1150 to 1300 was exceptionally warm, producing a degree of prosperity for farmers in northern Europe. The period from A.D. 1550 to 1770 is often known as the 'Little Ice Age', and it was a cold period which resulted in hardship for the people of the Alps and Scandinavia as local glaciers advanced and occupied previously cultivated land. The reason for these small but important climatic changes is still undiscovered, but it is a sobering thought that although it would take centuries – if not millennia – to produce an ice sheet over northern Europe and America we might see enough change in our lifetimes to affect our lives noticeably.

The temporary snow-cover that we receive in winter is an ephemeral but powerful warning from the realm of ice. That snow vanishes in warmer weather and the threat vanishes with it. It is only when conditions allow snow to lie unmelted all year round

that it develops its remarkable powers for self-compression and movement – powers that have made it such a potent sculptor of scenery. As snow falls year after year upon unmelted snow, it builds up to great heights and its weight begins to exert vast pressure on the lower layers. Under pressure the snow becomes ice and, as the pressure increases, the ice changes character. The end-product of this process is glacier ice which is so compressed that it is squeezed out from under the weight of snow piling on top of it, and this moving ice is the natural sculptor that slices with abrasive force at everything in its path. It gives some idea of the colossal weight behind the chisels of ice to know that over much of Antarctica the ice cap is many thousands of metres thick.

The erosion which is taking place in Antarctica can be appreciated from ice-carved landscapes in latitudes which are now ice-free. The Antarctic ice cap is so big that it would cover all 48 contiguous United States of America or all of Europe from the North Cape to Africa and Portugal to the Caspian Sea. But, during the last great Ice Age, North America was covered by an even larger ice sheet and this, as well as the ice which covered northern Europe, has left its scars. The beautiful Sognefjord of Norway is an ice-cut valley which compares with the Grand Canyon in scale as a physical feature. The great mountain ranges of the world have been raised by earth movements but they have been shaped by the grinding of ice – as the famous Matterhorn illustrates so perfectly. Although the great ice caps have gone from our temperate latitudes they have left behind many massive and beautiful glaciers – none more stunning than the Great Aletsch – which have their sources above the snow-line in the

high altitudes of great mountain ranges. These glaciers all have different characteristics but they are by no means immobile – the ice in some Alpine glaciers flows at a rate of several kilometres a year. It is the position of the glacier snout where the ice turns to melt-water that tells us how the ice age is progressing. If the snout is advancing down into the valleys the weather is becoming more severe, but, if the snout is retreating, it may be the effect of more benign weather.

We seldom realize how much ice has done to shape landscape. The Scottish Highlands cannot now boast a single glacier but much of their captivating scenery was sculpted by the last ice caps which disappeared 10,000 years ago. In the same way Wales, Ireland and the English Lake District can show many fine glacial features. So much of North America holds examples of glacial landscaping that it would be invidious to point to individual examples. The former alpine ice sheet formed the basin of Lake Garda in Italy as well as many other lakes and valleys for some distance all around the present alpine area. The effect of ice in these temperate zones has been so widespread that it is not difficult to find and it shows us what great changes may occur when the ice comes again.

Above: The slopes of Mount Paine in southern Chile have been scored by the marks of ancient ice floes. Above the snow-line ice still gouges away at this lofty peak.

73

The Matterhorn

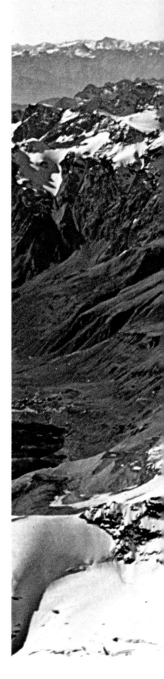

The Matterhorn is the most dramatic mountain peak in the world. It is a lone, challenging pyramid of rock in the Swiss–Italian Alps which has given its name to hundreds of summits of similar origin all over the globe. But, as the Matterhorn is the first and most famous of all horn peaks, so it is the most perfect and the most starkly unique. It has enough competition in the Alps alone from such famous mountains as the Jungfrau, Mont Blanc, and the Eiger while in the Himalayas, mighty Everest itself is a horn peak. But the Matterhorn is cleanly etched, alone and majestically uncluttered by subsidiary peaks.

All great mountains seem to have a 'pull' which leads to drama and tragedy. The Matterhorn can claim one of the most distinguished victims to have perished because of an obsession with it. This was Perren, one of the most famous of pre-war Alpine guides, who was known as 'the wolf of the glaciers' by his whimsical compatriots. Most of us would be happy to climb a mountain once, and others would find satisfaction after a dozen assaults, but Perren would not retire until he had climbed the Matterhorn 150 times. As he grew older his strength and skill diminished and finally his luck failed and he fell to his death six climbs short of his target.

The Matterhorn is a sheer pyramid of rock because it has been carved by chisels of ice. Indeed, the reason for the steep, forbidding peak of some mountains is the gouging of great glaciers which have transformed it from a pleasantly rounded summit into a sharp horn. This process is carried out not so much by the river glaciers themselves but by their sources in the valley heads among the great frowning mountain tops. Here the sheer weight of unmelted snow which falls year after year feeds the stupendous ice rivers known as glaciers. The snow presses down on its lowest layers until these layers become ice and then presses even harder until this ice becomes plastic and is squeezed out from under the titanic weight of the ever-increasing snowfall. This ice is pushed out in all directions and, although most of it will roll down the path of least resistance and form a glacier, some of it will be continually wearing and tearing at the retaining walls of the surrounding mountains which contain it. In time these valley heads will become deep recesses – amphitheatres closed in on three sides by rock walls and finding their only release in the fourth side which is the point the glacier starts from. When they reach this state the valley heads are called cirques (unless you are English in which case you will call them cwms from a Welsh word pronounced coom, or corries in the Scottish vernacular).

Where the glacier meets the head wall of the surrounding cirque, colossal forces will be brought to bear. Alternate freezing and melting will chip at the rock while the remorseless, grinding pressure of the weight of ice eventually proves irresistible. The cirque wall becomes steeper and steeper and is worn back centimetre by centimetre. All mountain tops which are above the summer snow-line are above the point at which they can gain much relief from the constant pressure of the snow melting. Above the snow-line the weight of falling snow increases and can only be relieved when the ice squeezes a way out and down the mountain side. In these high places there will often be many cirques gradually enlarging and working their way towards each other. The cirques not only drive their head walls back but they make them steeper and steeper until, if they

Left: The symmetrical eminence of the Matterhorn. This famous horn peak has an awesome, three-sided pyramidal shape.

work from both sides of the mountain range, they reduce the central part of the range to a sharp-crested, jagged ridge called an arrêt.

Eventually even the arrêt gives way before the assault of the ice. The first notch in it will permit the two cirques to join forces and is called a col. This is only the beginning as the ice gradually erodes the weaker, lower parts of the head wall and the cirques move toward the highest and strongest point. This point –

the last bastion against the levelling ice – will be a sharp-pointed pyramidal peak known as a horn.

So the drama and beauty of the Matterhorn is not some delightful freak of the mountain building process. The stark perfection of its cruel peak is the result of constant sculpture by the grinding force of ice. It is the supreme and original horn mountain – lovely, lonely and challenging.

Sognefjord

Beneath the dark, waveless waters of Sogne-fjord lie still, terrifying depths. The walls of this, the greatest of Norway's sea inlets, plunge as much as 1219 metres (4,000 feet) below the level of the surface. Above the water the sides of this 180 kilometre (112 miles) long flooded valley slope steeply up another 609 metres (2,000 feet) before the rise becomes more gentle and resolves itself in a plateau from which occasional mountains tower up to 1370 metres (4,500 feet). The average width of the fjord is only five kilometres (three miles) and it runs through wild, bold and barren scenery to cut its groove through the highest area of Norway. There are over half a dozen branches to the Sognefjord and some of them are at least as impressive as the main channel. On the south side lies the famous Naeroyfjord which, for most of its length, is far narrower than the height of the 609 metre (2,000 foot) cliffs. To look straight up at the towering cliffs from the deck of a ship cruising down the Naeroy-fjord is an unforgettable experience.

The visual beauty of this northern water-way can be overpowering. Its terrific length and high, towering sides can have a claustro-phobic effect and its mood changes with the light and the weather. Because it is so far north and because its high walls throw long shadows, it is usually seen in twilight and because of its moist atmosphere, it is often misty. Combining the features of mountain and coastal scenery in a thinly populated country, it is mysterious, forbidding and solitary. For most of the year it is shrouded in that famous Nordic gloom which gave birth to the doomed gods of Nordic legend – gods who feast in Valhalla with the heroes before their final defeat and the cataclysm that will overtake the world. Sognefjord saw the sails of Viking ships and it is still easy to imagine those fierce raiders slipping through the still waters bent on their dark and bloody purpose.

The Vikings may well have become seafarers because of this environment. The great, steep-sided gash which the Sognefjord cuts through Norway makes travel and communication across it peculiarly difficult. Even today the sheer fjord walls offer little purchase for roads and although one runs halfway along the northern side of the main Sogne-fjord, most of the roads in the fjord system merely run down to the heads of the various branches. The shoreline villages of the fjords are linked by boat services which connect at the junctions of branch fjords rather like a railway system. Even these connections are made in an unusual manner. The steep sides and great depth of the fjord preclude the building of a pier or harbour and the bottom is too far away for the small ships to drop anchor, so they simply tie up to each other.

To the Norwegians a fjord is a word for an arm of the sea but, because of the rugged nature of the coast of Norway, it has come to mean something more to geologists. Norway is so indented by long, narrow channels of the sea that its shoreline runs for 19,312 kilometres (12,000 miles) to cover a headland-to-headland distance of only 2,735 kilometres (1,700 miles). These coastal indentations have high, steep sides and where they bend or branch, they do so at sharp angles. Because of these striking characteristics geologists apply the term fjord to similar features in other parts of the world. There are plenty of them, but nearly all are in latitudes higher than 45 degrees which provides some evidence that fjords were created by ice. Indeed, one can still see ice-filled fjords in some places. Greenland's magnificent Søndre Strømfjord

Above: Steep sides loom over the still waters of Sognefjord. A glacier 1,370 metres (4,500 feet) thick cut this great gash through Norway's highlands during an ancient ice age.

has a glacier pouring right down to its end where blocks of ice 'calve' off to form icebergs on the fjord's chill waters.

Some geologists are not completely satisfied about the ability of glaciers to carve these massive flooded valleys out of the hard rocks of the fjord lands. There is ample evidence that glacier ice is very plastic and easily flows round any obstacle so that it is not as efficient an agent of erosion as might be thought. Besides this, great troughs, such as the Sognefjord, have been scooped out well below sea-level. Although ice floats, ninetenths of it remains submerged. As we know that sea-level was within 91 metres (300 feet) of its present depth during the ice ages, the Sognefjord glacier would have had to have been 1,370 metres (4,500 feet) thick to have

Left: Sognefjord shrouded in mysterious Nordic mist. The deep trench of this ice-cut sea inlet has always proved a formidable obstacle to Norway's land communications, and the small ships which navigate its waters find few landing points on its steep sides.

done its work. Nor have all glacierized coast-lines produced fjords: Scotland has fjords, known as lochs, on its west coast but none on the east which was very heavily glacierized and made of similar rock.

Despite these objections the connection between ice and fjords is clear – whether glaciers gouged out the whole valley from scratch or whether they trimmed the shape of earlier, water-cut features. All the fjords are on coasts backed by upland areas which carry, or once carried, great ice caps. The colossal weight of snow on these stationary ice masses squeezed plastic sheets of ice down the slopes towards the coast and gradients separated them into individual valley glaciers each carving its own hollow. This ice was thick enough at Sognefjord to cut out even that massive trench and there is still a shallow bar or threshold across the mouth of Sognefjord which marks the spot at which the ice floated up and calved off the great glacier. Similar thresholds are common to most fjords. Now the great Norwegian ice cap which produced such mighty glaciers 10,000 years ago has melted away, leaving only isolated ice sheets such as the Jostedalsbre. When the ice was at its thickest, however, it packed the North Sea and constrained the ice flow from the Scottish Highlands which explains why the east coast of Scotland does not boast the fjords of the west.

The fjord phenomenon is widespread. Greenland, North America, Iceland, New Zealand and Chile are some of the many countries which have fjorded coastlines but Norway is the country which gave a name to the geographical wonder and to the Sogne-fjord, greatest of Norwegian sea inlets, with its chill, dark waters sheltering beneath its towering sides.

79

Dachstein and Paradise Ice Caves

Above: The underground glacier in Austria's Dachstein cave is decorated by large, but fragile looking stalagmites. Sadly, the movement of the glacier will eventually destroy them.

We all know what delightful decorations ice can make. There are the intriguing patterns that frost makes on a window pane, the clear beauty of icicles and even the satisfying reflection of the warm, amber colour of a glass of whisky and ice. The loveliness of caves is less widely appreciated as exploration of most of the world's huge kingdom of underground chambers and labyrinths is restricted to hardy enthusiasts. Caves, nevertheless, are often very beautiful, particularly where they are decorated not only by stalagmites and stalactites, but also by the less well-known calcite helictites, screens, straws and columns. Indeed, some caverns are so lofty and so ornate that one cannot help but make a fantastic comparison between them and the finest cathedrals raised by man. When the rich splendour of this underground world has the pure, hard beauty of ice added to it, it provides a magnificent spectacle. Some of

the greatest ice caves could almost be the setting for the fairy-tale Ice Palace conjured up by the master story teller Hans Christian Andersen.

There are two types of ice cave. Some, like the famous Austrian ice cavern of Dachstein, are simply ordinary limestone caves which have become decorated, indeed, covered, with ice because of their low air temperature. Others are hollowed out of glaciers like the Paradise caves of Mount Rainier. The extraordinarily fine Dachstein cavern contains a miniature underground world with a myriad of delicate decorations. Massive ice stalagmites and translucent ice curtains adorn the underground glaciers covering the entire floor of this enormous cave which has been etched into the limestone. For tourists the entrance to the cave is situated high up on the mountain face and at the site a cable-car has been specially built to transport visitors up to it.

The existence of permanent ice in a limestone cave is surprising. The cutting out of limestone into caves depends upon the eroding and absorbing effects of water as it filters or runs through limestone. Ice does not filter anywhere and it does not absorb limestone. The reason is that the temperature inside the limestone itself remains fairly constant, summer and winter, at around the freezing point of water. This enables water to percolate through the limestone and it is only on contact with the air within the main cave system, which is below freezing except during high summer, that it begins to freeze. The air within the main system is at such a low temperature because cold air sinks and warm air rises, which is of crucial importance to the ventilation of many caverns. The constantly

low temperature within the Dachstein cave occurs because it is so high above sea-level. Its lower entrance is below the snow-line but the weight of the cold air inside the cave draws more freezing air down from narrow fissures in a high cold plateau, which, though too narrow for man to enter, form the top end of this super-ventilator. And when the air current is reversed in winter and the air outside is colder than that in the cave, even the air drawn in through the lower entrances is below freezing.

The caves in Paradise glacier on Mount Rainier in Washington State are of pure ice, not ice-decorated limestone. Mount Rainier is crowned by no less than 14 glaciers and, although they all undoubtedly have holes of some sort in them, the Paradise glacier has produced the most spectacular and accessible caves. The creation of pure ice caves is not unlike the creation of limestone caves. Water seeps into the glacier through the cracks or crevasses in its face and begins to melt the ice below its surface in the same sort of way as it wears at subterranean limestone. Passages and chambers have been created under the surface of the Paradise glacier but these are obviously not on the scale of some of the

Above: Icicles form on the ceiling of the Dachstein cave and join the glacier's slowly moving ice. Just below them a few small ice stalagmites have formed.

enormous underground limestone systems.

The Paradise caves are only a temporary phenomenon. Although they have certainly existed on something like their present scale for at least 15 years, the internal movement of the glacier is constantly distorting them and will eventually destroy them. Glaciers are sensitive to the friction of their beds. This means that the ice in the centre of the stream moves more quickly than that at the edges. In addition to this, the ice at the bottom of the glacier is held back by the rock and moves more slowly than the less restrained ice above it. These internal movements warp the ice caves and the general movement of the whole body of the glacier is downwards towards its melting point where the whole structure will be destroyed.

Indeed, destruction is all too commonly the fate of both sorts of ice caves. So many cave decorations are unbelievably fragile – mere tracings or patterns of ice – that the slightest change in their equilibrium can damage them. Obviously, a drastic, internal change of temperature would make considerable changes in any sort of ice cave, but it is the ice-decorated cave which is particularly at risk. When one considers that the limestone around the Dachstein cave is usually at a temperature only slightly above freezing point and that it is the cold air within the cave that actually freezes the water that emerges from the roof and walls, it is evident that a fairly delicate balance exists. This balance can easily be upset by human interference. Obviously such massive chunks of ice as the glacier within the Dachstein cave will not be affected, but there are decorations in certain ice caves which are so delicate and so ethereal that they can be damaged by the mere passing of human bodies with the consequent warm-

ing of the cave atmosphere. Luckily, most cave decorations are more robust and measures have been taken to protect those decorations which are obviously at risk.

Paradise and Dachstein are splendid examples of the two different sorts of ice cave. Of the two, the interior of the Dachstein is probably the more richly varied, displaying a great range of ice formations copying their calcite brothers and then outshining them.

The Paradise caves have a certain rarity value, however, as one's appreciation of the caves is deepened by the knowledge that, while natural forces are constantly increasing the size and complexity of the system at Dachstein, they are moving relentlessly to reduce the Paradise caves to melt-water. There remains the sure consolation, however, that there must be many more equally spectacular caves awaiting discovery.

Above: The main passage of the Dachstein cave. Deeper inside there is an underground glacier. Left: An ice cave marks the mouth of a tunnel formed by melt-water from an Alaskan glacier.

The Great Aletsch Glacier

The Great Aletsch glacier is the mightiest of Alpine ice-rivers. From its lofty summit on the Jungfraujoch to its snout in a wild gorge below Bel-Alp it forms a solid, 27 kilometre (17 mile) long mass of ice which fills a valley that is three kilometres (two miles) across at its widest point. This great valley glacier is continuously moving as a semi-solidified torrent through the intoxicating scenery of the Bernese Alps. The snows on the incomparable 4,166 metres (13,670 feet) high peak of the Jungfrau provide its source and it ends, after winding for so many kilometres and receiving other ice-rivers as tributaries, when it finally melts into water.

It seems mysterious how such a rock-like, tooth-smashing substance can move sinuously down a valley's curves. The idea that glaciers were on the move has long been understood. Early experiments showed not only that ice moved, but that it moved in many ways just as water did in a river – the middle of the glacier travelled faster than the sides and the ice on the outside of a bend moved faster than that on the inside.

This is because the underside of glacier ice is very different from the brittle ice of indoor skating-rinks. The glacier's source is in the great mountain bowls or cirques above the snow-line where snowfalls over many years press down heavily on the existing ice and snow. Under these pressures ice crystals develop and are able to move over one another a trifling distance; when this slight movement is repeated billions of times by the countless crystals, even in a small volume, the pressurized ice has become quite fluid or plastic. For various reasons this plasticity is increased when the crystals are all lined up pointing in the same direction and this is precisely what happens to them when they come under great pressure. So the compressed, fluid ice on the bottom begins to be squeezed out of the cirque or basin, which is the source of the glacier, by the sheer weight of the snow above it. As it goes down the glacier valley it carries many metres of less compressed ice above it, and this top layer, being more brittle, is less well adapted to coping with the ups and downs, the twists and turns, of the glacier's course. When the glacier comes to a sharp dip in its valley, great cracks or crevasses appear on top of the ice as it slides over the lip of the step. These cracks are often squeezed shut when the glacier's course levels up again. The Great Aletsch glacier is extremely heavily crevassed along its sides where the upper ice has been splintered as its edges were slowed down by friction against the valley walls. Crevasses can be 61 metres (200 feet) deep and pose a hazard to climbers and skiers.

The Great Aletsch and all valley glaciers constantly wear away at their beds. The ice scoops rocks and dirt from the sides and floor of its channel and drags them down to its snout like a great file. The abrasive effect of these constantly moving ice giants is colossal and many of the deepest and most dramatic of the world's valleys and fjords were gouged out by glaciers which existed in the Ice Age. This habit of tearing at the confining rock and transporting it along has some delightful visual effects. The sides of a glacier collect a lot of rubble from the rock walls so that, where a tributary joins the main glacier, the junction of the two streams is marked by a dark band (moraine) that continues the length of the glacier, where the two edge strips of rubble have merged but not mixed in with the ice due to its relative stiffness. This can be seen where the Middle Aletsch glacier grinds

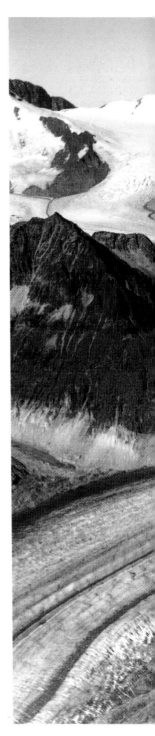

Above: The Great Aletsch glacier in all its majesty, as it flows round a bend in its course. The dark, regularly spaced lines of medial moraines follow every movement of the ice.

which runs away in a torrent from the bottom of the glacier and, by their reflection of the sun, help to give that vivid blue-green colouring to any Alpine lakes that contain such water.

On its 27 kilometre (17 mile) course the Great Aletsch glacier forms a dam which confines a beautiful lake called the Märjelen See. The body of ice in the Great Aletsch is so mighty and weighs so many tonnes that it appears to be an unburstable dam. However, as the waters of the Märjelen See increase with the combination of rainfall and melt-water, they approach a critical point after which they escape in a rush through the crevasse systems and ice tunnels in the glacier. In the past this dark triangular lake regularly produced violent and dangerous floods. This problem has now been averted by the success of an ambitious and expensive project which involved the drilling of a tunnel through the rock side of the lake so that it can no longer overfill, thus flooding the surrounding terrain with its accompanying disastrous consequences.

There is no doubt that the Great Aletsch glacier is beautiful but it is also an example of one of the inexorable forces of nature. Glacier ice combines the virtues of brittleness and plasticity to overcome all obstacles. The brittleness continually erodes its rock sides while the plasticity helps it to adapt to writhing around the hardest and highest rocks in its path. The weight and strength of its onslaught are such that one can imagine no man-made structure that could withstand it. The sheer tonnage of a 27 kilometre (17 mile) long river of moving ice, 3 kilometres (2 miles) wide in places and as much as 500 metres (1,600 feet) thick makes a battering ram that no amount of ferro-concrete can survive.

down from the Aletschhorn and joins the Great Aletsch; the dark bands of the medial moraines below this point are as regularly spaced as cart tracks, following every curve in the ice and clearly showing that the Middle Aletsch is not the first major tributary that the Great Aletsch glacier has received. In these moraines and on its side and back the Great Aletsch not only carries great boulders but lots of finely ground rock flour. These tiny particles are suspended in the melt-water

Snow Avalanches

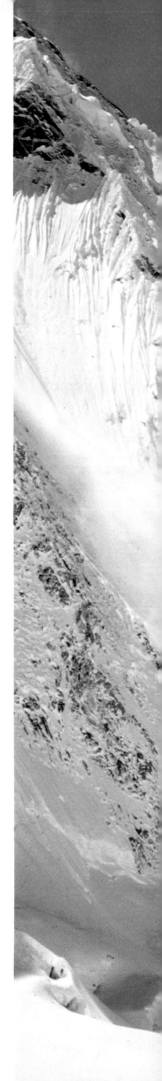

The avalanche has fully earned its grim title of the 'white death'. Year after year avalanches reap a staggering toll in human life and yet, through ignorance, they are consistently underrated. They can move at speeds of over 320 kmph (200 mph) when they become airborne and the explosive blast of their passing can flatten vast expanses of sturdy forest and annihilate villages. One of the most destructive and murderous avalanches of all time, the 1962 Santa Valley disaster in Peru, killed 4,000 people and 10,000 animals, flattened six villages and damaged three more while it ran for 16 kilometres (10 miles). Many of the casualties resulted from a flood caused by the overflow of the temporary lake which had been dammed up by the avalanche. Such monsters are uncommon but lesser avalanches are not – the Swiss Alps alone have a total of around 17,500 reported avalanches a year, probably making them the most common phenomena of the mountains. The enormous danger which the unwary risk on mountain slopes that are prey to avalanches means that more victims will be claimed every winter.

Avalanches are not in reality caused by their own spite but by the nature of snow crystals. Over 6,000 different types of snow crystal have been discovered so that the subject is very complex, but the basic form of crystal is a tiny hexagonal plate which grows as it falls through the moisture-laden atmosphere. When snow settles on the ground it starts to undergo a number of changes which, if they continue unchecked by melting or avalanche, will result in glacier ice. This process is called firnification. First of all a new fall of snow settles under its own weight and becomes firmer and more cohesive while a large amount of air is expelled by its mass. The upper layers of snow, which are in

contact with the cold mountain air, are colder than the snow at ground level which remains at or near freezing point. The crystals in the lower, warmer areas continuously give off water vapour which is recrystallized above. The bigger crystals develop in a certain layer and, in so doing, develop large intergranular spaces which give the layer an extremely low strength and allow subsequent layers to slide off them.

There are a few extraordinary factors which may cause instability in a bank of snow. It can, for instance, lie on a slippery slope, such as one covered in long grass. Then, when the snow begins to melt, the water percolates down and lubricates the grass so that the snow is ready to slide off it. At other times wind packs the snow in dense, hard masses whose crystals are already so damaged by the gale that they will not settle much after they have landed. If these wind-blown drifts land on looser snow which is still settling, a gap will open between the two layers leaving a perfect and deadly booby trap for anyone who steps on to the apparently firm surface.

There are nearly as many different sorts of avalanche as there are different snow conditions. Ground avalanches can occur with both wet and dry snow and even on the slightest slopes of ten degrees. In the Alps, each spring produces many huge and well-known wet avalanches which follow recognized avalanche paths. Ground avalanches should never be underestimated because they are frequently deadly, but they cannot travel as fast as the more spectacular airborne avalanche. This appalling menace occurs when any loose dry-snow avalanche reaches a critical speed somewhere around 80 kmph (50 mph). At this point the friction along the bottom and sides of the snow mass will cause

Left: Given the changeable nature of snow crystals, avalanches are to be expected on these steep mountain-sides although they can occur on slopes which are as slight as ten degrees.

enough turbulence to throw it into the air after which it can achieve colossal speeds in excess of 160 kmph (100 mph) and also give a blast effect, like a high explosive bomb, beside its course. The blast effect occurs because the snow particles drag a huge amount of air with them and this swirls out of the body of the avalanche at about twice the speed of the snow.

The avalanche seems sometimes to lie in wait for its prey, and therefore the superstitious think that it has a mind of its own: some members of a party can cross a dangerous slope before the avalanche is triggered off by the last few people, sweeping them to their deaths. In the Middle Ages there were legends that avalanches were caused by witches, and folklore often personifies the avalanche into a fiendish being: 'Was fliegt ohne Flügel, schlagt ohne Hand und sieht ohne Augen?' (What flies without wings, strikes though it has no hands and sees without eyes?) runs the old riddle and the answer is 'das Lauitier' (the avalanche beast).

Whatever form the avalanche takes, it is a fearful sight. It can come rolling majestically with a sound like thunder or it can come shrieking in a smothering, white blanket. Even tiny avalanches can kill and they hold their victims so tight that bodies have been recovered which have been unable to move under a mere metre (three feet) of snow. It is this extraordinary, changeable nature of snow which causes the phenomenon. It can be firm one minute and treacherous the next. It can be a loose, tumbling mass, but will set like concrete around its victim. It is a fascinating and unique substance and it is at its most dangerous in the avalanche.

Icebergs

Above: At the height
of summer most of
the Antarctic is still
covered in glacier ice.
The ice is slowly
squeezed out towards
the sea to form shelf-ice
before being broken
into icebergs.
Right: An Arctic
iceberg towers out of
the sea.

These huge, silent, white monsters ghosting through the oceans are a lethal hazard for shipping. This has been the popular view of icebergs ever since the 'unsinkable' *Titanic* was detroyed on her maiden voyage. The popular view is not so far wrong. Icebergs come in enormous sizes and they can last in the sea for years drifting to unexpected places. An Antarctic iceberg sighted in 1956 was nearly the same size as the country of Belgium at 335 kilometres (208 miles) long and 96 kilometres (60 miles) wide. The tallest iceberg spotted originated in Greenland and

towered over 152 metres (500 feet) out of the water. Another one from the Arctic was spotted in 1946 and was still floating about in 1963. Icebergs are the biggest floating things on the planet – no super tanker can ever match them – and as nine-tenths of the ice is hidden under water they represent many tonnes on the move.

It is no accident that the Antarctic has produced the biggest iceberg and the Arctic has produced the tallest. This is because Greenland and Antarctica have very different coastlines. The iceberg is no broken piece of

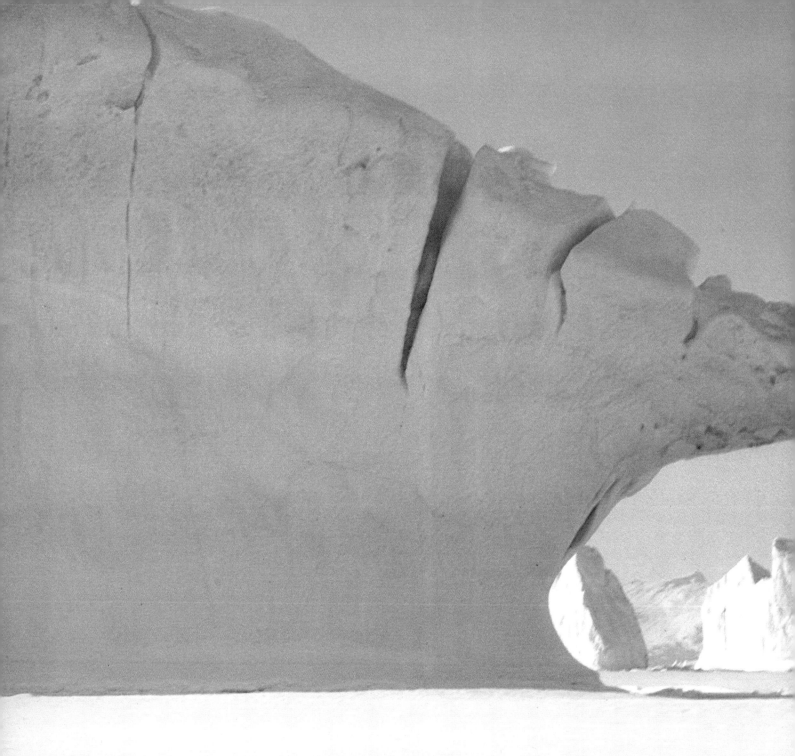

Above: Greenland's ice-covered cliffs cause the 'calving' of tall icebergs. In this picture icebergs can be seen floating away from the shore's steep outline.

pack ice but the very special product of an ice cap, which can only exist over land. On permanently frozen land masses, snow accumulates to such depth that considerable pressures build up in its lower layers. The sheer weight of falling snow compacts that which lies beneath it until it forms the purest pale blue, translucent hard ice. The pressure on this ice keeps growing as the snow piles up and eventually it begins to move. Ice may seem to be fairly rigid material but extreme pressures make it plastic – almost fluid – and it becomes squeezed outwards in all directions from the centre of heaviest pressure.

It is when this ice reaches the seashore that its shape as an iceberg is decided. In Greenland it is likely to cascade downwards through gaps in the cliffs. When it reaches the sea it becomes water-borne because it floats. This means that long tongues of ice project out from the land and are pushed upwards by their buoyancy. Eventually, they are bent up too far and they come away with a crack. This is called 'calving' and it can sound like thunder or gunfire. In the Antarctic the coast shelves very gently into shallow water so the ice can push out many tens of kilometres before its buoyancy makes it break away.

Since the tragic loss of the 'good ship *Titanic*', icebergs have been cast in the public imagination as the villains of the polar seas, to be most carefully avoided. In this concern we can overlook their grandeur and immense beauty, and forget that their presence is an essential component in the maintenance of the world's climatic system and its equilibrium. Old icebergs, doomed as they are to die in an inhospitable environment, become more and more interesting as they age; as they drift about the oceans, the air temperature is often warm enough to melt the exposed ice faster than that underwater. When this happens the ice floats higher out of the water and sometimes shows fascinating wave-cut caves and platforms.

Icebergs from both north and south travel into unexpectedly warm latitudes. An Arctic iceberg has been spotted as far south as Spain while one that originated in the Antarctic has reached the latitudes of South Africa. The iceberg can be a thing of remarkable beauty as it floats silent, glittering, vast and immensely dangerous on its random course.

THE
FACE OF
THE WATERS

Life on Earth depends upon water. Of course water is not the only essential, as oxygen, sunlight, temperature and many other factors are required to support fragile life. Without water, however, nothing grows and nothing eats and the astonishing thing is that there is so much water available but that it is so badly distributed. Over 70 per cent of the Earth's surface is covered by the seas and oceans and these contain 97 per cent of all water. The remaining 3 per cent is freshwater of which 77 per cent is locked in glacial ice. Some glacial ice is extremely useful and provides a frozen reservoir which feeds vital rivers as it melts in the dry season, but most permanent ice, 74 per cent of all fresh water, is held by the unproductive Antarctic ice cap. With 22 per cent of fresh water circulating at various depths below ground, there is only a paltry one per cent in lakes and rivers. There is so little water vapour in the atmosphere that, if it all fell at once in an evenly distributed shower, it would produce only a few centimetres of rain. Yet despite the small proportion of water which flows over the land area at any given time, it is nature's chief eroding agent and largely responsible for shaping the exposed surfaces of our continents.

The oceans were born as soon as the Earth was cool enough and the atmosphere stable enough to contain them. Early accretions of water which may have existed in a vaporous envelope about the planet would have been swept away when the sun 'came to life' and started radiating energy. Water was given off, however, by the partial melt beneath the surface of the young Earth and, as conditions favoured it, this water from within the planet began to accumulate. As the crust solidified, the low-lying regions, between the isolated continental blocks of granite rock, filled up with water to form the oceans. These consisted of salt-water almost from the moment they formed because they contained chlorine which was also given off from within the Earth and sodium which was a by-product of the weathering of rock.

Once the oceans had been born they began their invaluable contribution to the support of conditions favourable to life. The most obvious aspect of this contribution was as a great reservoir from which the sun's energy could draw up water vapour to be distributed by the winds of the atmosphere and precipitated over dry land as rain and snow. Many of us take this beneficial circulation of rainwater for granted but it is erratic. In one area, such as the Amazon basin, rainfall can be so great that it leaches vital minerals from the soil and produces easily the largest river in the world while, in other areas, life may be hard or impossible to maintain owing to the near perpetual drought. The great ocean masses also make a significant contribution to an overall stability of temperature which rivals that of the atmosphere. The ocean currents, such as the Gulf Stream, undoubtedly play a part in exporting heat from the tropics to more temperate areas. But ocean currents are so numerous and so complex that their effect upon our climate has never been fully evaluated. It is possible that a slight change in the course or strength of these currents is the switch that will trigger off a new ice age but, at the moment, such ideas are pure speculation. What is certain is that the oceans are not static but provide a delicate regulating mechanism for the world's climate.

Despite its fragility, the vagaries of the global climate do present us with a temp-

tation to meddle – especially where there is a shortage of rainfall for irrigation. Australia is a prime example for, although it is a prosperous, food-exporting country, certain physical features make the vast potential of the continent unrealized or even un-realizable. Northern Australia receives a monsoon in the same manner as the immensely fertile countries of southern Asia but, because Northern Australia has no backing of high mountains to catch the rain, its fertility is limited. In the same way the vast area drained by the Murray-Darling river might be as fertile as the valley of the Mississippi if its rainfall and irrigation were

the same. If a tiny fraction of the world's fresh water were directed to the ideal places the political picture of the world would no doubt be very different. But the natural system of water distribution would be hard to improve upon on any appreciable scale without major technological developments. This is unfortunate because it would take very little of the available water resources to irrigate huge deserts – indeed it is a source of wonder that the fresh water which makes up the most stupendous waterfalls such as the thundering Iguaçu, the greatest lakes and the grandest rivers is drawn from 0.03 per cent of the world's entire water supply.

Above: A picturesque view of Lake Muncho in Canada. Water forms lakes, seas, rivers, snow on mountains and ice at the North and South Poles. It covers about three-quarters of the Earth's surface.

The Dead Sea

The Dead Sea is the lowest lake on Earth by quite a margin. Anywhere else which is more than 91 metres (300 feet) below sea-level is covered by water, but the surface of the Dead Sea and its surrounding shores are 393 metres (1,290 feet) below sea-level and its waters are as much as 398 metres (1,300 feet) deep in places so that rock-bottom is 792 metres (2,600 feet) below the Mediterranean waves. The Sea is maintained and fed chiefly by the River Jordan. The Jordan is not one of the largest rivers in the world, being no more than a rapid, muddy stream about 27 metres (90 feet) across in its lower reaches and between one and three metres (three and twelve feet) deep. Yet this river, together with one or two insignificant streams and springs, is enough to pour six and a half million tonnes of water into the Dead Sea each day in certain seasons (attempts at irrigation may have affected this total over the last two decades) but of all this water, none ever flows out of the Dead Sea. The level is controlled by evaporation caused by the high temperature of the Jordan valley during most of the year and this means that all the salts, silts and chemicals which its tributaries bring into the Dead

Right: The dry rugged landscape around the Dead Sea. The remains of a first-century Roman fortress are still clearly identifiable. Below: Cracked saline deposits surround the Dead Sea.

Sea remain there while the water does not.

The resulting high level of salinity has given the sea its name and reputation. Its total salt content approaches 25 per cent compared with the 4 to 6 per cent for ocean water. In appearance the water is deep blue and very calm. The calmness is a result of the solids in solution and therefore the water is so dense that swimmers always float. No fish live in the waters and it is devoid of life save for a few single-celled organisms which have adapted to its hostile environment. The Arabs maintained that its waters gave off such nauseous fumes that no bird could fly across it and live. This does not seem to be true and the area even has its own bird, the charming swallow called Tristram's Grackle (*Onchagnathus Tristramii*) which is unique to the Dead Sea. Human beings who bathe in the saline waters do so without harmful effect although they acquire a temporary, salty crust.

It would be difficult, however, to find a stretch of water as small as the Dead Sea which has more legend or myth associated with it. It is 75 kilometres (47 miles) long and 16 kilometres (10 miles) wide at its widest. This stretch of water is closely associated with the cautionary story of the cities of the plain and Lot's wife. The cities of the plain were Sodom and Gomorrah which are still bywords for vicious and sinful living, although the details of their sinfulness is left to the imagination. The cities might have been spared from their fate if ten just men had been found within them but the populace was evidently so given over to its undefined lusts that only Lot and his family were given a warning of the wrath to come. As they fled from the scene, fire and brimstone rained down on Sodom and Gomorrah and Lot's wife did the one thing which the angels of the Lord had forbidden her to do – she looked back. She was turned into a pillar of salt and, interestingly enough, the area to the south of the Dead Sea abounds in salt pillars.

The reason why the Dead Sea is the lowest lake on Earth is still a matter of some controversy. The Jordan valley is in the

Above: The extensive saline deposits clearly visible in the foreground give an idea of the Jordan Valley's intense heat which evaporates much of the Dead Sea's water.

northern part of the Great Rift Valley and there is much learned argument about how or why the Great Rift Valley was formed. The faulting of the Earth's crust which caused this great trench started before the Cretaceous Age 70 million years ago, but the present-day Dead Sea is a later creation and probably not more than 12,000 years old. It is a strange sea in a desolate and inhospitable place. Parts of its shore resemble the waste from a chemical works with untidy heaps of bitter, saline residue. In the midst of this and nearly always shimmering in the intense heat is the blue lake itself into which so much water runs and from which nothing flows.

The Great Barrier Reef

The mighty chain of the Great Barrier Reef which fringes the east coast of Australia is the biggest and richest single bank of coral in the world. There are other barrier reefs in the Indian and Pacific Oceans, but for sheer size and variety of coral species and formations the Great Barrier Reef stands alone. It stretches an incredible 1,930 kilometres (1,200 miles). Its southern tip is on the Tropic of Capricorn just north of Brisbane and it loops up in a great arc around its own coral-bound sea past Cape York, the northern tip of Australia, and westwards to the Gulf of Papua, overlooked by the jungles of New Guinea.

The incomparable size of the reef is due to the various geographical conditions which have combined to make the Australian coast an ideal habitat for coral. Coral can only live in a very special environment: namely warm, clear, shallow, turbulent, salty water. It must have warmth and one of the necessities of its life is water which never cools below 22° C (72° F). This means that it is restricted entirely to the seas of the tropical regions. The water must be clear, as mud would block the coral's digestive system and kill it. It requires shallow water where there is plenty of sunlight to stimulate plant growth which is the first step in a food chain that produces the coral. It is significant that shallow waters also provide a turbulent zone where there are breaking waves to give a well-oxygenated water essential to the coral's survival. The adult coral lives a static life attached to the reef and cannot swim into more congenial waters as a fish can, but must rely upon a plentiful supply of oxygen in its permanent environment. The Pacific rollers, breaking on to the wide continental shelf of North Australia,

therefore provide the optimum conditions for a reef. In addition, fresh water means death to coral, which explains why early navigators and explorers always found a break in a reef opposite a river mouth when they were trying to land on the Pacific islands. The Australian coast is kind to coral in this respect as well, because no major rivers drain to the seas of the Great Barrier Reef Province.

Coral has been growing on the Pacific shore of Australia for hundreds of thousands of years. This accounts for the size of the Great Barrier Reef compared to the tiny atolls and lesser reefs which surround oceanic islands where the deep waters prevent any wider expansion of the coral. It is not just the size of the Great Barrier Reef that makes it remarkable but the richness and variety of its coral types. Fortunately the coast of north-eastern Australia is in a peculiarly advantageous position to attract a wide variety of coral species. Coral, in its adult form, is firmly anchored to its place on the reef, but its young or larvae can be swept considerable distances by currents. The Great Barrier Reef is in waters with access to both the Indian and Pacific Oceans and so forms a point of settlement for coral species typical of each. The importance of this is emphasized when a comparison is made with the Indo-West Pacific Ocean area where there are more than 500 species of reef-building coral while the Caribbean can boast no more than 50. This is because the land barriers of America and Africa, tipped as they are by cold seas, prevent coral larvae from passing between the two areas.

The construction of the Great Barrier Reef is the result of an amazing and complex natural phenomenon. Anyone who has ever

Above: Erskin Island, one of the Capricorn Islands in the Great Barrier Reef Province. The tiny island is surrounded by a wide expanse of coral reef.

seen a coral reef will never forget the staggering impact of bright colours and strange, delightful shapes made nearly fantastic by the presence of many sorts of fish and sponges. It is not easily apparent that the brilliant, living coral is growing upon the heaped-up bones of the dead. Most people could be forgiven for imagining that coral was a form of plant life for certain species resemble seaweeds and they all live out their lives tethered to one spot upon rocks or shells. However, despite the fact that coral is wonderfully varied in colour and shape, the anatomy, structure, life-style and habits of every species classify coral inescapably as a member of the animal kingdom. For example, most plants draw their energy from the sun by the process of photosynthesis, but coral feeds as animals do. The breeding habits of coral also betray an animal nature. Besides this, each little coral animal can respond to stimulation by moving about inside the limestone cup or skeleton that it builds for itself, while plants can

usually only respond to stimulation of various sorts by changes of growth.

In recent years the reef has been ravaged on an unprecedented scale by one of coral's natural predators, the Crown-of-thorns starfish (*Acanthaster planci*), due to a sudden increase in its population which may be the result of man's activities. It is likely that human interference in the form of oil spillages and chemical effluents could be disrupting the ecological balance and thus affecting the Crown-of-thorns' breeding. It is also possible that the depredations of the starfish on coral communities is simply a natural and recurring problem which has only been noticed because of recent scientific

investigations, but studies of the Crown-of-thorns' life-style nonetheless continue.

It is the limestone skeleton of the coral which holds the secret to its reef-building habits. When each coral animal's span of life is ended, it dies but leaves its skeleton behind as a limestone anchorage for more coral to grow upon. So the Great Barrier Reef is, in essence, a great heap of countless millions of calcareous skeletons upon which the living coral is growing. It is impossible not to be awed by the continuity and achievement of these little animals when one considers that the Great Barrier Reef alone occupies a sea area of perhaps 259,000 square kilometres (100,000 square miles).

Above: The varying blueness of the sea gives a good indication of its relative depth. Here waves break on the shallows of the Great Barrier Reef.

The Maelstrom

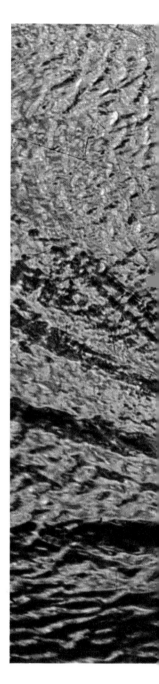

Maelstrom has been accepted into the English language as a synonym for turbulence or confused violence. It originates from the Moskenstraumen, a strait through the chain of Norway's Lofoten Islands which has a reputation for whirlpools and dangerous, boiling seas. Near the middle of this terrifying channel but towards its eastern exit lie the shoals of Herjeskallen over which the waters bubble and seethe even in good weather, while bad weather causes waves to break over them. The whole stretch of water has been made famous by Edgar Allan Poe's imaginative description of it:

'the smooth, shining and jet-black wall of water, inclined to the horizon at an angle of some forty-five degrees, speeding dizzily round and round with a swaying and sweltering motion, and sending forth to the winds an appalling voice, half shriek, half roar, such as not even the mighty cataract of Niagara ever lifts up in its agony to Heaven'.

Poe was an acknowledged master of Gothic horror stories and his account is a trifle fanciful but the Maelstrom is bad enough and impressive enough to be internationally famous.

The idea that whirlpools were caused by water running out through some hole in the sea floor was widespread and the Moskenstraumen strait was long supposed to be of unfathomable depth. Sadly for romantics, however, the very deepest part of the strait is 36 metres (120 feet). The Maelstrom appears to have been named by the Dutch from *malen* (to grind) and *stroom* (current) and it has been well known since medieval times, first appearing on Mercator's *Atlas* of 1595. Whirlpools have always been dreaded, and Homer's *Odyssey* included the terrible monster Charybdis who caused whirlpools.

Although a whirlpool's action is not caused by water gurgling through a hole, it does owe much to the shape of the sea bed. The Moskenstraumen channel is about eight kilometres (five miles) wide with a bottom of rock and white sand which is very irregular and rises rapidly from westward to eastward. As tides sweep across the North Sea to and from the coast of Norway, this narrow channel, even more pinched than it appears by a substantial bank on its southern side, becomes a bottleneck through which the mass of water is squeezed. Once through the strait, the water whirls around Vestfjorden inlet off the mainland coast of Norway, forcing its way back through Moskenstraumen even while the mainstream in the centre of the channel is still flowing strongly eastwards. At one-quarter rise of the tide all the water in the channel flows eastwards, but the water to the north and south is moving slowly while the mainstream in the centre is racing through. At half-tide rising the sea to north and south has already turned and begins to flow westward while the centre stream is still forcing through to the east. When the side and mid-channels are flowing in different directions like this, violent turbulence with swirls and steep, heavy, breaking seas occurs on both sides of the mid-channel stream. At about three-quarters rise of the tide, the mid-channel stream turns clockwise with great turbulence to join the others in flowing west.

The opposite occurs as the tide goes out. Obviously this remarkable state of affairs makes the Moskenstraumen a terrible proposition for a small boat, especially near the Herjeskallen shoals which constantly seethe with white water as the fast-flowing stream

Above: A dangerous whirlpool is formed where two conflicting currents meet in the Maelstrom. At the height of its fury the Maelstrom produces several different whirlpools at the same time.

is deflected upwards by rocky interruptions in its course. But there are times during which freak weather and tide conditions whip the Maelstrom to unequalled frenzy. It seems unlikely, but to quote the *Admiralty Pilot*, Volume III: 'It often happens in winter that, whilst a westerly gale at sea sends in a heavy westerly swell, there is clear weather over the land and a steady easterly wind in Vestfjorden; when this occurs Mosken-straumen is especially dangerous, for the meeting of the swell from westward and the sea caused by an easterly wind, combined with a strong stream, causes the whole channel to break across, and the stronger the stream the more violent the turbulence'.

The extraordinary way in which the Maelstrom seems to be divided into three different and sometimes conflicting streams is absolutely unique. That it is caused by the shape of the channel and the conditions in Vestfjorden inlet into which it runs is accepted, but no hydrologist has done enough work on the area to enable a detailed explanation of the mechanics of the phenomenon. No technical explanation would, in any case, subtract from the awesome reputation of this seething, turbulent stretch of water with its vicious currents and whirlpools.

The Amazon

The Amazon is the world's largest river. It is such a giant that the world's next largest river – the Congo – discharges less water than just two of the Amazon's tributaries, the Negro and the Madeira. Rivers twice as long as the Hudson are unmapped tributaries of the main Amazon river. There are claims that the Nile is the longest river in the world at 6,670 kilometres (4,145 miles) to the Amazon's 6,448 kilometres (4,007 miles), but even this can be disputed now that the Aswan High Dam has cut out a few kilometres from the Nile's meandering course and if the Amazon is measured as a continuous water-course through its complex delta region. What is not in dispute is that the Amazon is bigger than the Nile by volume. At the Amazon's mouth, one-fifth of the total river flow in the world is poured out, driving the salt sea-water back over 160 kilometres (100 miles). Even that statistic does no justice to the primacy of this mighty river because, owing to the flatness of its basin, it contains at any one time, two-thirds of all the river water in the world. When one thinks of the celebrated rivers of Europe, the mighty floods of India and China, the torrents of Africa and the great rolling expanse of the muddy Mississippi, combined with countless other streams containing only half as much water as the Amazon basin, it is apparent that the Amazon is built on a different scale.

The Amazon's great size is indicated by the existence of an island about the size of Switzerland in the gaping 320 kilometre (200 mile) wide mouth. If the left bank of the Amazon estuary ran through London, its right bank would be somewhere near Paris and it spews out 198,000 cubic metres (7,000,000 cubic feet) of water per second into the Atlantic when it is in full spate. In the vast and complex network of rivers which supply it, no fewer than 17 of its tributaries are longer than the Rhine.

The Amazon was discovered in 1499 by Vicente Yañez Pinzón – a Spanish sea captain who had been with Colombus on his great voyage. Pinzón was sailing out of sight of the coast when he discovered that he was voyaging through fresh water. He moved shorewards to investigate and anchored in the mouth of the vast river. In 1541, an expedition led by another Spaniard, Francisco de Orellana, travelled up the river and, among other things, claimed to have had an encounter with an Indian band whose most formidable warriors were tall, naked, white, long-haired women – so the river was named after the Amazon warriors of antiquity.

One of the most intriguing things about the Amazon is that its tributaries are distinctly different colours. The true source of the main river is 5,240 metres (17,199 feet) up in the Peruvian Andes and this starts off as white or dirty yellow. All the tributaries to the Amazon which run through the Andes are similar in colour as they carry heavy quantities of whitish soil in their waters. Various tributaries which originate in northwest Brazil and Venezuela, as well as a few which rise south of the main river, are apparently black in colour. In fact, these rivers are very clear and dark red because they flow over ancient, bare rock formations and are relatively free of sediment but heavy with iron. The mighty Negro is a black-water tributary and its waters can still be distinguished 80 kilometres (50 miles) downstream of its junction with the white torrent from the Andes.

Any effort to explain why the Amazon is

Right: An aerial photograph of the Amazon as it loops its way through Brazil, cutting a path through dense tropical forests.

Left: The expansive waters of the Amazon. Although named when a sixteenth-century expedition alleged that ferocious white female warriors lived along its banks, such reports have never been authenticated.

such a monster among rivers requires a study of the geological history of the American continent. A land mass of continental size is bound to be drained by great rivers and the natural pattern is for these rivers to radiate in all directions as they do in Asia. North and South America are different because high mountain ranges give them watersheds along their west coasts. This is because the Earth's surface is covered by a dozen or so great rafts or plates of almost rigid rock which are moved and ground against each other by very slow convection currents rising from the Earth's molten core. The North American plate and the South American plate are being pushed steadily westwards so that they ride over their neighbouring plate, which is the floor of the Pacific Ocean. This gradual movement of the American plates over the Pacific has built up the great chains of the Rocky and Andes mountains. These mountains just about cut off the west coast of the Americas and force the rivers to flow east to the sea.

The Amazon basin is also restricted to north and south. The highlands of Venezuela and the Guianas form a great semicircle to the north and the old, hard rock of the Planalto de Mato Grosso stands high in southern Brazil. This leaves just one low-level exit for the whole vast drainage area and that is the one the Amazon takes. To add to this natural concentration of most of the continent's drainage, South America enjoys massively heavy rainfall. The interiors of other continents harbour great deserts but the Amazon basin is in the right latitude for heavy, persistent equatorial rain. Circumstances have combined to give the Amazon the world's largest river basin and a wet climate. The result is the king of rivers.

The Iguaçu Falls

'After seeing Iguaçu Falls, it makes our Niagara Falls look like a kitchen faucet', said Eleanor Roosevelt. She must have seen this wayward giant at the right time of year because it varies in performance from a peak at which it discharges twice as much water as the Niagara to something rather less. The Iguaçu River which, in part, runs along the border between Brazil and Argentina, courses through a tropical belt of extra-ordinarily high rainfall – some 30 centi-metres (150 inches) a year – and obviously the seasonal variations of this immense downpour have some effect on the Falls. This is not to say that the Iguaçu are 'flash' falls which only achieve their peak when briefly and suddenly swollen by a cloudburst. The rainy season occasions a gradual and steady increase in the volume of water passing over the Falls, which reaches about 4,740 cubic metres (167,500 cubic feet) per second for 80 days at a stretch. However, South America is a land of mighty rivers and thundering torrents and the Iguaçu occa-sionally outdoes itself and flings 12,740 cubic metres (450,000 cubic feet) of water over the Falls every second. Its thunder, audible 24 kilometres (15 miles) away, has been silenced at least twice in living memory by a circumstance that is almost beyond belief – the lower river into which the water drops some 76 metres (250 feet) on a four kilometre (three mile) front has flooded until it has risen to the top of the Falls.

Such startling statistics would seem to guarantee the Iguaçu the position of the greatest falls in the world. Such a choice is a personal matter because many different superlatives come into the argument. The highest falls in the world are South America's Angel Falls – named after the American pilot, Jimmy Angel, who discovered the waterfall in 1935 after he had crashed his plane nearby – but these are a mere trickle compared with the titans of quantity. As far as quantity is concerned, South America triumphs again with the mighty Guayra or Sete Ouedas Falls which, in flood, are ten times as great as Niagara. But the Guayra are divided into 18 separate cataracts which are broken up and therefore lack a single great leap or drop. The greatest width of plunging white water in the world is at the Khon Cataracts in Laos which extend for 12,800 metres (42,000 feet) and are second only to the Guayra in volume. However, the Khon also lack any great drop and are more justly entitled cataracts than falls, al-though they certainly provide a stupendous spectacle. It all depends on what constitutes a great waterfall and, on this point, one should take into account those factors which make falling water so uniquely impressive. A very high but thin fall accentuates the height of its cliff rather than overwhelming the spectator's sense with the sound and sight of water. On the other hand, mere volume or width of surging cataract may be awesome enough but it lacks the majesty of a real fall in which a great, sheer curtain of water drops lazily into a cloud of spray with a roll of continuous thunder. That is the sight which provides the unique attraction of a mighty waterfall and, when it is at its peak, that is the sight which the stupendous Iguaçu provides on an unrivalled scale.

Oddly enough, primitive man has shunned waterfalls. To him such powerful natural phenomena were obviously the dwelling places of local deities or supernatural crea-tures. The Scandinavians thought they were haunted by trolls and demons and the

Above: Huge brownish curtains and columns of water pound into white spray and foam against the brilliant green backdrop of the jungle. The Iguaçu Falls in spate can easily equal and often exceed Niagara Falls.

Japanese also believed that demons provided the roar of the fall. The Indians of Canada dared not look upon the Churchill Falls in the last century because to see them was to die. The Africans regarded the Victoria Falls, the 'smoke which thunders', with awe and seldom visited it. The story goes that the local Indian tribe offered human sacrifice once a year to the spirit of the Niagara Falls but there is certainly no proof of this. What is more certain is that the power and danger

evinced by the roaring waters has provoked dark thoughts in civilized man; Conan Doyle's fictional creation Sherlock Holmes, most cerebral of detectives, so far forgot himself as to indulge in a vulgar brawl with his adversary Moriarty above the Reichenbach Falls. The sensational nineteenth-century tightrope walker, François Gravelet, alias Charles Blondin, made a spectacular crossing of the Niagara Falls in 1859. In front of a huge crowd he crossed over on a 335 metre (1,100 foot) high wire suspended 49 metres (160 feet) above the roaring waters. He later repeated the act with such variations as stilts and blindfolds.

When the first missionaries arrived at Iguaçu Falls they piously named the great cataract Salto de Santa Maria, but the local Guarani or Indian name, Iguaçu, meaning simply 'great water' endured despite their efforts. The very first Europeans to arrive in this part of South America learnt much from the indigenous Indian population and they cleared the forests by Indian methods, using fire and then planting their crops such as manioc (cassava). There was even a degree of intermarriage and ancient Indian customs such as free reciprocal aid for special operations like harvesting were adopted and are still practised to some extent today.

The spirit of the Iguaçu Falls must certainly be a benevolent one, however. During the days when bandit-soldiers of Iberian origin roamed South America kidnapping Indians as slaves, the Iguaçu provided a barrier to them. It became impossible for the Indians to live in villages or settlements within reach of the slavers who used the waterways of the continent to travel out on their forays. While they were unable to surmount the Iguaçu Falls, some devoted Jesuits were able to establish Indian settlements in security above them. But the bandits eventually worked their way around the unnavigable waters and attacked the settlements, carrying the survivors off to an extremely harsh life. Despite these regrettable incursions, the benevolence of the Iguaçu Falls had given the Indians 150 years of respite from the extension of hostile European civilization.

National parks have been set up by the

Argentinian and Brazilian governments on both sides of Iguaçu Falls and many modern hotels have been set up nearby to cater for visiting sightseers. The Argentinian national park was started in 1909 and, apart from providing a recreational area of great natural beauty, it also serves as a nature reserve to protect much exotic wildlife such as toucans and iguanas. It covers an area of nearly 520 square kilometres (200 square miles) and the Iguaçu Falls are its most spectacular feature. Although Iguaçu is most accessible by air, many visitors prefer to view the waterfall after a journey by boat down the picturesque Paraná river, of which the Iguaçu is a tributary.

Iguaçu Falls have sometimes been enthusiastically spoken of as a magnificent potential source of hydro-electric power. Apart from the obvious factor that there is as yet no immediate local demand for such a great supply of electric power, the project would require complicated co-operation between the governments of Argentina and Brazil. The venture would also need to overcome the problem of Iguaçu's changing volume of water since the Falls do not receive a regular and sustained amount of water from the erratic Iguaçu river.

Although they are no longer of importance as the guardian of an Indian sanctuary, the Iguaçu Falls provide one of the grandest sights in the world. They can be seen in all the glory of their primitive setting of dark green tropical forest glistening and dripping with the constant spray. The monstrous anger of the flood, the rainbows shimmering in the mist and the dark secret places behind the falling curtains of thundering waters are all a delight to the observer and a sombre reminder of nature's power.

Left: An awesome volume of water drops over the Falls on the Iguaçu river every second. In times of exceptional flooding the lower river can actually fill up to the lip of the Falls and silence their thunder.

The Sea's Tides

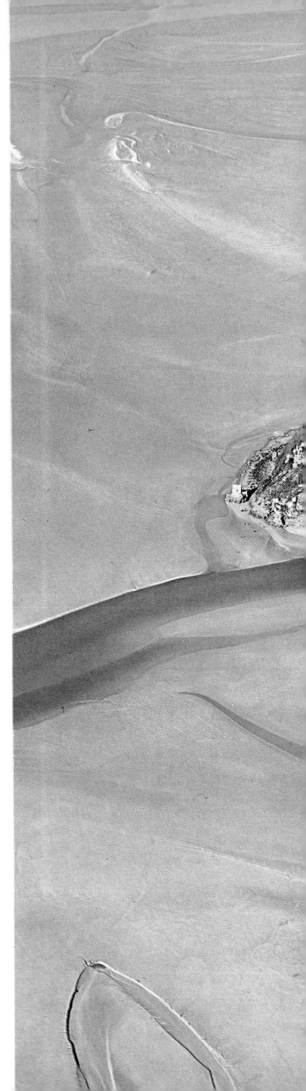

Tides very nearly ruined the British expedition of that well-organized soldier Julius Caesar. He and his forces were accustomed to the negligible tides of the Mediterranean and they therefore did not beach their ships adequately when they raided Britain in 55 BC. A high tide in the English channel, accompanied by a storm, caused severe damage to the Roman fleet and Caesar found himself in the position of a man temporarily without support or escape. The tide does not make much difference on the shores of Caesar's native Italy but in some parts of the world, such as the Severn estuary in England and the Bay of Fundy in eastern Canada, sea-level has been known to vary by more than 15 metres (50 feet) between high and low tide.

These huge 15 metre tides would have a very marked effect if they were experienced on every coast. The water would retreat many kilometres at low tide leaving enormously wide beaches. Harbours would need deep channels and long flights of steps to make them usable at all times. Even an ordinary tide ranging over six metres (20 feet) is enough to cut off islands at high tide but leave them stranded on the beach at low tide. An example of this is Mont St Michel in France. The local variation in the size of tide around an ocean's shores is due to certain geographical features. The Bristol Channel, which leads to the Severn Estuary, and the Bay of Fundy both have a tapering shape. The large quantities of water which are swept between their arms by an incoming tide are pinched to an ever increasing height as the corridor of the bay narrows. It is the funnel shape of the coastline, therefore, that produces in these instances record-breaking tides.

Right: The rock of Mont St Michel becomes an island at high tide, although it can be reached dryshod at low tide. It has long been the site of a picturesque and famous monastery.

It is, however, a question of scale which makes Mediterranean tides so much less significant than tides on the shores of the great oceans. Because of the relationship between the Earth and the moon, sea-water is banked up in two great bulges on opposite sides of the globe and these bulges remain almost stationary while the Earth rotates. This does not mean that half the Pacific Ocean drains into the Atlantic and vice versa each day because the waters of the world engage in a form of motion which can be compared to that of railway cars when they are shunted by a locomotive. Each freight car stops when it hits the buffers of the next car which is then impelled to move until it hits the next in line. The great open sheets of water behave in just such a way when they hit the barrier of a land mass. When this happens in the Mediterranean, tides are restricted to a metre (three feet) because there is not enough water in that sea to shift around and cause much difference in sea-level. The long, slow swell of the tide as it crosses a vast ocean such as the Atlantic produces a much greater effect upon the ocean seashore.

High tide occurs twice a day over the face of the Earth. As tides are caused by the pull of the moon and the Earth revolves once a day, it is perhaps to be expected that high tide should occur only when the moon is roughly overhead, that is once a day. In fact one of the bulges of sea-water which causes a high tide is a result of the gravitational pull of the moon and is on the side of the Earth facing the moon. The bulge of water on the other side of the Earth is due to a different force – the centrifugal force of the combined Earth-moon system. If you seize a bucket full of water and whirl around with it at the

full extension of your arm, the water will remain in the bucket owing to centrifugal force. The centrifugal force exerted by the Earth spinning on its axis is evenly distributed about the equator and so causes no bulges of sea-water. Although we are accustomed to think that the moon hurtles around the Earth, for the purposes of centrifugal force we should regard them as one entity turning end over end along their axis. Due to the relative weights of the two bodies, the centre of gravity of the Earth-moon axis is located inside the Earth but well over towards the side the moon is on. The centrifugal force of this system, acting upon the sea's water, is outward and greatest at points furthest from its centre of gravity – that is to say on the surface opposite the moon. This explains the second bulge.

The rhythm and size of tides are made even more complex by a number of other factors. The effect of the sun's gravity is not so pronounced as that of the moon, but it is not inconsiderable. The action of total centrifugal forces rather than just those of the Earth-moon system also has an effect. All this is further complicated because neither the moon's orbit about the Earth, nor the Earth's orbit about the sun is a perfect circle: the pull of both moon and sun is appreciably greater when either body is at its closest to Earth. There is also a considerable variation between tides when the moon and sun are aligned, and therefore pulling in tandem, and the lesser tides that occur when moon, Earth and sun form a right angle. As a further complication, the height of the moon above the horizon, its declination, also has to be taken into account. Once every 1,600 years all three heavenly bodies are lined up at their nearest with the moon at its highest and this

great occasion is marked by the greatest possible tidal range. It last occurred in the seventeenth century and produced disastrous flooding in Holland which caused whole villages to be washed away – even now, the flat landscape bears trace of the inundation.

The cause and effect of tides is a truly vast subject. Although the world's oceans are more obviously affected by the pull of moon and sun, the entire body of the globe feels their gravity to a lesser extent. The distortion which tides cause in the Earth's shape produces fractionally more friction, which retards its rotation. This means that, at a hardly noticeable rate, days have been growing longer. There is evidence that 370 million years ago the day was only 21.9 hours long. Such change would be imperceptible over thousands of generations.

The so-called 'tidal waves' that can cause so much destruction are sometimes thought to be caused by tides. In fact,

Left: As ocean waves run up the beach into shallower water, increased friction with the sea bed causes them to grow higher and topple over. This breaker is just about to crash on to the shore and seethe forward to the strand.

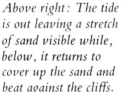

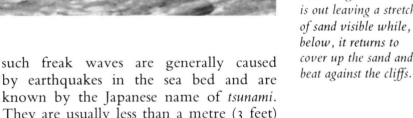

Above right: The tide is out leaving a stretch of sand visible while, below, it returns to cover up the sand and beat against the cliffs.

such freak waves are generally caused by earthquakes in the sea bed and are known by the Japanese name of *tsunami*. They are usually less than a metre (3 feet) high in the open sea, but they then build up towards the shore and can wreak terrible havoc. In 1964 an earthquake in Alaska generated *tsunamis* which reached California in nine hours and Australia in 20 hours, having travelled at a speed of 500 kilometres (310 miles) per hour.

The ceaselessly changing tides create a special habitat for the fascinating plants and animals of the seashore who have adapted to cope with either land or water and the shifting frontiers between them. The delicate ecological balance of these communities is permanently affected by the rhythm of the seas, and tides have greatly influenced our lives too. They have even influenced the physical make-up of our cities and coastlines, such as at Venice and Mont St Michel.

117

THE FIRMAMENT ABOVE

The wonderful or extraordinary sights that appear in the atmosphere are part of a set and ordered pattern. Our skies can seem impossibly turbulent and unpredictable, but in fact many of nature's more amazing expressions, from the violence of the hurricane to the wild beauty of the Aurorae, are part of a protective system that guards life on our planet. This system is the thin skin that the envelope of the atmosphere throws around the Earth. The upper limit of the atmosphere, where it is very tenuous, is only 1000 kilometres (620 miles) out from the Earth's surface and the densest region, the troposphere, is only 10 kilometres (6 miles) deep. This invisible surround of gases, water vapour and dust particles does an essential job in cutting out harmful radiation from the sun and determining the temperatures of the world at ground level. The winds and storms that we experience may seem to form a random pattern but they are part of an overall system that maintains a delicate balance of climate.

Although these atmospheric wonders stand out for their curiosity, beauty or dramatic power, they are all illustrative of an unsuspectedly orderly organization. Some of them are concerned with clouds and water vapour which not only take vital rain across the globe but have a decisive effect on ground temperatures by determining how much direct sunshine will reach the Earth and how much heat will be reflected back, through or past them. It is astonishing, when one considers what an immense variability there must be from day to day in amounts of cloud cover, how unvarying overall temperatures are. The awesome hurricane gives some indication of the immense power locked in the fragile atmosphere. Whirl-

winds and lightning are not freakish hazards but the result of certain conditions that arise during the complex workings of what is, in essence, a sensitive machine which maintains life-supporting conditions over much of the Earth's surface.

Since the atmosphere is a delicate mechanism, there is much concern that it may be affected by pollution. There are a number of ways in which human activity may affect our climate and the best-known is probably the 'greenhouse effect' of excessive carbon dioxide. Our respiratory process uses up oxygen and produces carbon dioxide but any imbalance that this has caused in earlier times has been righted by the photosynthetic processes of green plants which absorb carbon dioxide and give off oxygen. However, once the Industrial Revolution gained momentum, the increased burning of fossil fuels such as coal and oil meant that more oxygen may have been used up and more carbon dioxide produced than members of the plant kingdom could cope with. As carbon dioxide is a very efficient absorber of long-wave radiation from the sun this could mean that the lower atmosphere will grow gradually warmer. This overheating would lead in turn to all sorts of disasters such as the melting of polar ice caps and consequent flooding when sea-level rose. Although this disaster is a very realistic possibility it is only right to point out that many years of strenuous industrial activity have not yet resulted in a marked change of global temperature.

Of almost equal concern is the possible effect of dust and other particles belched into the air by chimneys and exhausts. The resultant haziness has, first of all, affected cities which tend to have more cloud than surrounding rural areas. But the constant production of pollution-laden air has begun to affect areas far removed from industry so that a marked increase in haziness has been noted from an observatory in Hawaii. These particles in the air reduce the amount of solar radiation that can reach the ground and could result in an overall decrease in temperature. Although there is no immediate cause for alarm it is, perhaps, time to realize that the firmament above us is a fragile and vulnerable thing. For all its occasional displays of destructive force the atmosphere is not inimical to life but is indeed its protector. The refraction of light, the change of seasons and the circulation of water vapour may all produce unusual or striking effects but they are part of a natural balance which we must take care not to upset although we can continue to find out more about precisely how the atmosphere works.

Above: The fading light of a beautiful sunset makes the clouds seem darker and silhouettes the land. Some of the colours of the light spectrum are scattered by their long journey across the atmosphere but the orange and red bands still reach the ground and tint the sky. Previous page and left: Two dramatic evening skies which are both the result of the complex, but orderly, workings of the atmosphere above us.

The Rainbow

The rainbow's arch of seven bright bands of colour is a common and beautiful sight. It needs only the conjunction of sun and rain at the right angle for a rainbow to appear. Although most of us see many rainbows in our lives, there are rare occasions when, owing to meteorological circumstances, we see one of particular brilliance complete with faint inner bows and a secondary bow. It is always a pleasure to sight a rainbow and an unusually bright or complete one is memorable. Mostly a bow is a faint sheen of colour glimpsed amid the rainclouds but, at its best, it is so clearly defined as to seem almost solid. Because it is a commonplace phenomenon it is taken for granted. 'My heart leaps up when I behold a rainbow in the sky' wrote the romantic poet William Wordsworth about the pleasure most of us feel at such a sight.

The rainbow has been regarded as a lucky omen as well as a cheerful sight. The Bible describes it as a sign of mercy which God shows in the heavens to reassure us that, despite the rain, he does not intend to inflict a catastrophe like Noah's Flood upon us again. 'I do set my bow in the cloud and it shall be for a token of a covenant between me and the Earth', God promised Noah. There are some who believe that this is literally true and some who regard it as a charming explanation of a phenomenon – not understood by the authors of the Bible. It is also considered to be a lucky sign in Celtic mythology although the Celts obviously have a more venal idea of luck than the writers of the Scriptures. They believe that there is a crock of gold buried at the rainbow's end and all you have to do is dig it up to be rich beyond the dreams of avarice.

Every culture has ingeniously accounted for the rainbow's appearance and its intermittent existence. In Greek mythology, for example, Iris was the goddess of the rainbow and she also acted as the messenger of the gods. The Aborigines of Australia saw the rainbow as the rain's dutiful son whose bow was necessary to protect his father from falling down. They believed, therefore, that the brilliant rainbow should be driven away lest its efforts should cause a drought and they performed elaborate rituals to this end. Although western traditions generally regard the rainbow as a lucky omen, the Karens of Burma, for example, thought the rainbow was a malignant and dangerous

demon who devoured children, and the Zulus also feared the rainbow, associating it with snakes. Among some Polynesian peoples the rainbow was the path of heaven and Bifrost, the sacred bridge of Scandinavian myth, was a seven-coloured arc leading to the homes of the gods. At the time of Ragnarok – when, according to Norse belief, all things would be destroyed – the rainbow bridge would be broken under the weight of the giant Surt and his followers riding over it with swords drawn. Traces of belief in the sacred nature of the rainbow still survive in some country customs and children's rhymes.

In Europe this traditional apprehension of the rainbow survives. In the north of England, for instance, children still play at 'crossing out' the rainbow by placing two sticks crossways. Old methods of predicting the weather by the rainbow linger on in popular sayings such as 'a rainbow at night, the rain is gone quite'. Often such simple recommendations are proved to have a scientific basis.

The optimism of the Celtic myth may be justified but anyone who has tried to find the crock of gold knows that the rainbow's end is hard to track down because, however fast you move towards it, it still maintains its distance from you. It is impossible to reach the rainbow's end because the rainbow is an

Above: A rainbow sparkles over Victoria Falls in central Africa.

image. The arc we see is caused by the reflection and refraction of sunlight at a certain angle which means that the sun will always be behind the observer and the rainbow always in front. The sunlight is reflected in drops of rain and, as one advances on the bow, it will advance ahead by being reflected in different raindrops (the angle of reflection does not change). This means, in effect, that two observers standing side by side will be seeing a slightly different rainbow because the sun will be reflected to each by different raindrops.

The seven colours of the rainbow illustrate the fact that light is compound. We are all used to the idea of sound being on different frequencies and accept that dog whistles can be pitched too high for the human ear so that they seem silent to us although they can be heard by a dog with its higher hearing range. In the same way we know that radio waves come on different frequencies and we tune our radios in to different stations accordingly. Light is electro-magnetic radiation and it is not white as it seems to be but is a compound of the seven colours of the rainbow. When light is passed through a pair of angled transparent surfaces (such as the walls of a glass prism or the two sides of a raindrop) it can be made to bend just as a bullet might ricochet off a slanting surface.

As bullets of a different weight might ricochet at different angles, the seven light frequencies are bent at different angles and separated out. The result of this process, which is called refraction, is that light which has been refracted reaches us in a separated sequence of violet, indigo, blue, green, yellow, orange and red rather than all together in the compound which our brains accept as white light.

The intensity of the rainbow's colours depends upon the size of the raindrops producing it – the larger the drops the more brilliant the colours. A brilliant rainbow may well confuse us by being accompanied by a fainter, secondary bow in which the seven colours are ranged in reverse order. The secondary bow is caused by light that has been refracted twice which accounts for its comparative faintness. The secondary bow will appear outside the primary bow and be completely detached from it.

So there is no point in reaching for a shovel and rushing towards the rainbow's end when you see one. It is better and more restful simply to appreciate its beauty, which has lit up many a grey day, and experience the pleasure that this phenomenon inspires in its beholders.

Above: Rainbow effects on a stormy day near the English coast. Right: Primary and secondary rainbows. The primary bow is the brighter one on the left with its sequence of colours running from violet on the concave side to red on the convex. The secondary bow is fainter and the sequence of colours is reversed.

Cloud Formations

Clouds come in fascinating shapes. Most of us have been struck from time to time by the beauty or strangeness of some cloud formation. Very few of those marvellous sunsets which the tropics seem to produce so constantly would amount to anything spectacular without the dramatic, dark shape of flat clouds illuminated by the last, slanting rays of the sun. Clouds change their shape and colour from day to day according to the weather we experience and they are classified on this basis. A specific type of cloud goes with every type of weather. It is the weather system that is responsible for the type of cloud we see at any one time. Owing to the infinite variety and constant mutability of the world's climate, there are occasions on which very unusual or very splendid cloud formations appear.

There are only four main types of cloud. These are *cirrus*, the word coming from the Latin meaning a lock of hair; *cumulus* meaning a heap; *stratus* meaning a layer; and *nimbus*, the storm cloud. These terms are all fairly self-explanatory as cirrus are the thin, wind-drawn clouds occasionally known as 'mares' tails'; cumulus clouds are the fleecy, woolly ones piled high like a range of snowy mountains; stratus are the flat layers of cloud, which are always low and formless and when they break up they often become discs or lens-shaped patches; nimbus clouds are dark and billowing with stormy menace. These four main types of cloud are divided into 13 different varieties. They describe either crosses between the main cloud types or give the additional information that they are *alto* (high) or *fracto* (broken).

All clouds are moisture droplets suspended in the air. It is worth knowing, however, that not all airborne moisture is visible

and that it only becomes so under certain circumstances. Water evaporates into the atmosphere from a number of different sources. A great deal of moisture is given off by plants through the process of transpiration while geysers, volcanoes, power stations and even kettles all contribute. However, it is the heat of the sun upon the sea and other large expanses of water in the tropics which draws the largest quantity of water into the atmosphere. The warmer the air, the more water vapour it can contain and, when it reaches its limit, it becomes saturated but the vapour still does not become visible. When warm, saturated air cools, however, the water within it becomes condensed into tiny droplets which are held in suspension in the air. When this happens near the ground it gives rise to fog or mist, but when it happens as heated air cools upon rising to more rarefied heights, the condensed water vapour appears in the form of clouds. Under normal circumstances further cooling of clouds will lead to further condensation until drops of water form which are too heavy to be held in suspension and they fall to the Earth as rain. It is worth bearing in mind that cirrus clouds, among others, are often composed of super-cooled crystals of ice which are still fine enough to remain airborne.

Once clouds have formed they are shaped by prevailing conditions in the lower layers of the atmosphere. In this area the factors which can affect clouds are so complex that it is no wonder that weather forecasters have a high rate of error. At its very simplest, warm air caused by the direct radiation of the sun expands and bubbles upwards in the tropics. As this current of expanded air rises to a more rarefied plane it will bank up until it flows off into regions with less uplifted air,

Right: Cumulo-nimbus clouds such as these are created as moisture-laden air rises from the warm sea and condenses slightly in the cooler air above.

Above: The evening sky off the coast of Sweden. As the day closes and the sun sets, cooling begins and the clouds begin to flatten, thin out and eventually disappear.

that is polewards. As it does so, cooler air will be flowing in at ground level to take its place. In a static situation there would always be winds from the polar regions at ground level and airstreams pushing out from the equator at an upper level. However, the rotation of the Earth together with a host of lesser disturbing factors – such as the different effects of radiation on land and water and the upward flow of air over mountain ranges – combine to break the monotony of this pattern and give us the varied weather we know. The result of all this is that air con-

taining different levels of moisture will be pushed along in diverse directions at various speeds, unequal heights and all sorts of temperatures – resulting in contrasting cloud formations.

The most dramatic cloud formations are often caused by local, geographical differences. Major weather systems bring skies that are all too familiar but the upcurrent of air that flows over a mountain range, or even an individual mountain, can make cloud shapes or forms which are special. Such upcurrents give rise to spectacular wave clouds

that seem to follow the contours of the mountain peaks and this can be even more magnificent if layered cloud is forced upward so sharply that the various layers seem to be stacked one upon the other. The delightful nacreous or 'mother-of-pearl' cloud is formed when mountains force comparatively dry air up into the stratosphere where super-cooling will so reduce its power to retain moisture that some of the little moisture it contains will condense to form cloud.

Clouds are not always necessarily 'natural'

or beautiful to look at. Apart from heralding weather hazards, they often form over industrial cities where the air is polluted with sulphur gases. These clouds contain very dilute sulphuric acid, formed when the gases dissolve in water, and the acid can be carried for thousands of kilometres before it falls as 'acid rain'. A recent report by Swedish ecologists blamed such clouds from Britain's industrial cities for the mysterious death of fish in freshwater mountain streams and in Sweden's lakes. The scientists claim that acid rain destroys whole aquatic

Above: These cumulus clouds over the Caribbean are generally small and scattered. When clouds cluster like this more moisture-laden air is drawn up through their already moistened columns and they reach greater heights.
Right: A view of the evening sky in Sweden's lake district. Ecologists have become concerned recently about the pollutant effects of sulphur-bearing clouds.
Far right: Mares' tails. These cirrus clouds are composed of tiny ice crystals which are drawn out by the wind.

ecosystems from basic plankton upwards and that it can damage crop growth by taking mineral nutrients from the soil. Scandinavia is particularly vulnerable to these sinister clouds because the soil is lime-deficient and incapable of resisting acidic substances. Since the introduction of sulphur-free North Sea oil as an industrial fuel in Britain, however, it is hoped that the sulphur pushed into the atmosphere is decreasing and clouds are becoming more innocently beautiful again.

In many traditions clouds are associated with heaven and deities are imagined literally to live in them. The Greek and Hindu gods were fabled to reside at the peaks of Mount Olympus and Mount Everest respectively; both mountains appear to touch the sky and are permanently crowned by clouds. In popular Christian traditions and art, ascents to heaven are depicted with clouds as the bearers of saintly figures, such as the

Virgin Mary up to celestial heights.

Clouds are much more than a grand display in the sky, and they are more than the carriers of precious rain to irrigate fertile lands. They are an important part of the process by which the atmosphere evens out temperatures over the globe and widens the area on which life can flourish. Heat is not only exported from the tropics by winds and sea currents, but it is locked up as energy in the evaporation of water. When this water condenses again the energy is released as heat so the effects of some of the radiation that blazes down upon the equator can be felt in cooler regions. Besides this, cloud cover can protect the Earth's surface from the full force of the sun and also act as a blanket thus stopping heat from escaping into the upper atmosphere and then into space. Clouds are therefore an essential part of the complicated equation which keeps the surface temperature of much of our planet roughly the same day after day.

The Aurorae

The Aurorae are the most beautiful and mysterious of celestial phenomena. They are sometimes vast bands or arcs of light and at other times, dancing, moving rays. They may form great drapes in the sky which are bright enough to read by and their colours vary from greenish-white to blood-red or violet. They are common in both extreme northern and southern latitudes, but increasingly rare in temperate areas where their appearance can give rise to some anxiety. Demonstrations of auroral light over medieval Europe gave rise to legends of giants fighting in the sky and fear of flaming lances from heaven.

The simple credulity of medieval man has now been replaced by scientific dispute. This is surprising when one realizes just how often the lights appear. They only appear about four times a year in northern Florida, but they are visible from Churchill, Canada, for 300 nights in a year so scientists are not short of sightings or photographs and statistics. It seems from these studies that the Aurorae tend to occur with similar intensity at the same time in both northern and southern hemispheres, take different forms and colours at different heights and cover a colossal slice of sky. In 1959 an Aurora Borealis (Northern Lights) was measured at 4,828 kilometres (3,000 miles) long in an arc 160 kilometres (100 miles) high.

All Aurorae come from a long way up in the atmosphere but it is their height that dictates the sort of display we see from the ground. There are 12 reasonably distinctive sorts of Aurorae and they have all been measured at their own particular heights. It has been found that, on average, the more common forms of arc come from 69 to 104 kilometres (43 to 65 miles) up while the

distinctive draperies are 109 kilometres (68 miles) away and the highest displays are 997 kilometres (620 miles) from the Earth. There is some evidence that red-coloured lights are more common at greater heights and this is explained by the fact that the atmosphere is thinner there and so the charged gas particles in the upper region are less likely to collide with one another. When they do collide the particles lose their charge and thus the ability to radiate the light that we see. So the glorious Aurorae can be best understood scientifically as the shifting patterns of light which are only visible in the night sky in high latitudes.

The whole phenomenon of auroral light is explained in terms of the impact of a solar storm on the Earth's atmosphere. A flare emitted by the sun can release energy equivalent to one million large nuclear bombs and this can send solar particles hurtling through space towards us at the speed of light. The chief barrier to these particles is the Earth's magnetic field which curves out from Pole to Pole. As a result the field lies squarely across the line of solar particles heading for the equator or the tropics and deflects them. The highly charged solar particles crash into particles in the terrestrial atmosphere leaving them charged. (They excite atmospheric gases, too, which produce auroral light.) They can charge a number of particles in this way before they are exhausted. These terrestrial particles rid themselves of this charge by radiating which gives off the light that we see in the Aurorae.

So the beautiful, dancing polar lights are the delightful results of solar 'storms'. No scientific explanation can dim the wonder of a celestial event of such vast proportions. It is a transitory and changeable phenomenon which may brighten, fade or move across the sky but which is still spectacular and remarkable.

Above left: The Northern Lights on display over the Alaskan sky.
Above: Aurora Borealis is known as the Northern Lights. Displays of Aurora Australis occur in the southern hemisphere at the same time and about the same intensity as the Aurora Borealis.

The Tornado

The concentrated violence of the tornado demonstrates the elemental power of the wind at its most hostile. It reaches down from heavy clouds in a great, whirling spiral and, wherever it touches the ground, tears things apart or uproots them with a mighty force. A destructive tornado in action can amble along at 48 kmph (30 mph) making a noise as loud as an express train and leaving a 400 metre (1,320 foot) wide track of devastation. It can hit hard with winds of 320 to 480 kmph (200 to 300 mph) which uproot anything in their path and spew the debris out over an even wider area than is covered by the vortex. As the column of air which is the tornado rotates at speed, the air pressure at its centre is sometimes so low that houses caught in it literally explode from the pressure and suction of the air trapped inside them.

The whirlwind is synonymous with disaster and destructive power. 'They have sown the wind and they shall reap the whirlwind' prophesied Hosea in the midst of a

Left: A tornado threatens to damage buildings in Texas. Where the base of the whirlwind touches the ground it hurls dust and debris into the air.
Right: A waterspout is simply a tornado at sea. The long funnel is made visible by the condensation of water vapour within it and not by sea-water being drawn up inside it.

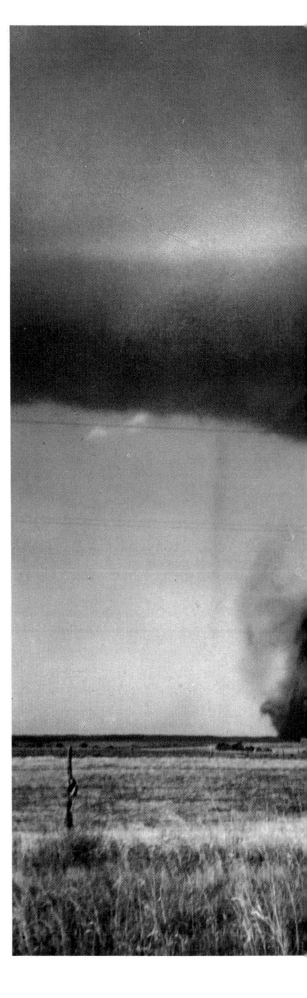

long string of blood-curdling threats against the children of Israel who had, once more, fallen from grace with God. To Hosea the whirlwind was just an expression of total calamity, an idea of stupendous, freakish force. To primitive man such a phenomenon was not only beyond his control, as indeed it still is today, but also terrifyingly beyond his comprehension. Sometimes after the waterspout has passed, the ground is left covered with small frogs or even fishes, and this was readily interpreted as divine retribution or some form of warning. It is still a rare and frightening thing for most of us, but there are some areas where it is a reasonably common occurrence such as the mid-western United States.

When the grey funnel of the tornado curves down from a huge, dark cloud, it is the result of unusual weather conditions. Cold, dry air behind a cold front can run straight into warm, moist air. When this happens the cold undercuts the warm air and causes it to bubble up producing convection clouds. If there is a stream of air at higher level this will pull the warm air up even faster to form towering clouds. Then a clearly defined funnel will grow from the base of the cloud towards the ground. This funnel is visible even before it is filled with dust and debris because the low pressure within it causes condensation. When this tubular vortex touches the ground there will be a disturbance of colossal violence. The tremendous winds, whirling in an anti-clockwise spiral, will snatch whatever they touch up into the air. When this happens over the sea there will be a waterspout, and when it happens over land it produces a tornado which appears the more dramatic

Right: The dark funnel of this tornado reaches down to track across the dusty prairie soil of Oklahoma. Tornadoes are relatively common in the American mid-west during spring.

136

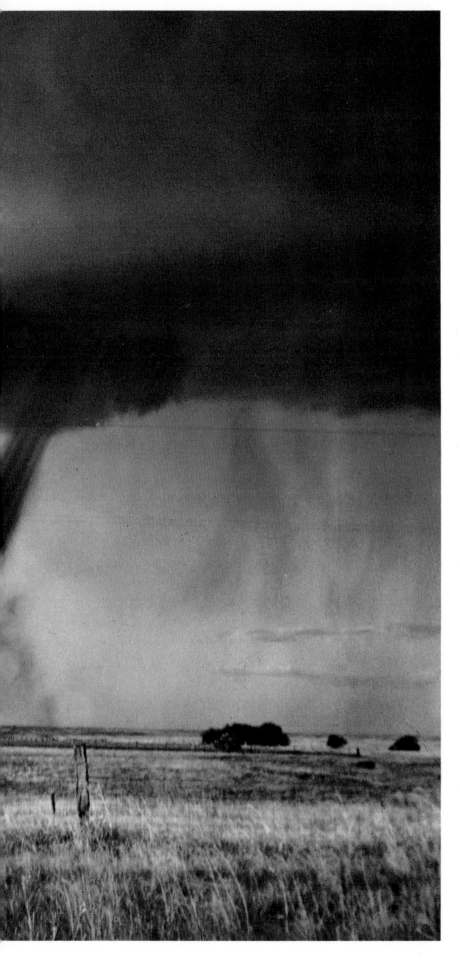

the more dust and rubbish it can throw about.

Fortunately the weather conditions necessary to produce the whirlwind are rare in most places. The exception is North America in spring and early summer. During these seasons cold fronts from Canada push south and may clash with warm, moist air from the Gulf of Mexico which is flowing north. The United States experience about 150 tornadoes each year. The states most regularly affected are those which border the Mississippi and those of the mid-west of America. Many farms in these areas have tornado cellars which provide shelter from the advancing tornado. Although a single tornado can pass after a short time, they often occur in groups with tragic results. In 1965, for example, 200 people were killed in the mid-west by a group of tornadoes. Parts of the Soviet Union and Africa can also be seriously affected by tornadoes with the associated hazards of desert sand-storms and funnels of dust. Tornadoes can crop up in the most unlikely places. Although they are usually very weak in Europe, they can still ruin crops and trees and even Britain – not noted for climatic extremes – has been scourged occasionally by an isolated tornado.

The wreckage-choked column of the whirlwind is the most dramatic demonstration of the power of the elements. Although it can and does cause destruction and death, the carnage is usually confined to a comparatively narrow, short track. It will deploy the matchless violence of its 480 kmph (300 mph) winds and explosive low pressure along that track, but it cannot match the wide area of destruction that a hurricane or typhoon leaves. It is wind at its most concentrated – a whirling funnel of frightening power.

The Midnight Sun

The difference between summer and winter becomes ever more dramatic closer to the Poles. In the depth of the Antarctic winter, day is indistinguishable from night. The sun simply does not rise and there is total darkness in the Antarctic circle. At this time the Arctic circle is enjoying its high summer with the sun visible for 24 hours a day. This state of affairs gradually changes so that six months later it is the Arctic that will be plunged into darkness and the Antarctic that will be bathed in sunlight.

The sun is so necessary for warmth, light and life itself that people become more sensitive to the seasons the nearer they are to the Poles. Because the growth cycle depends upon the strength of the sun, crops can only be grown in the short summer and the long winter can be a hard time. When the dead, dark, gloomy season of winter in the colder latitudes is contrasted with the beautiful, leafy summer, it is not surprising that the appearance of the midnight sun gives rise to celebration and some strange customs. The stirring of sap in plants and trees touches an answering chord in human consciousness and midsummer's day is celebrated with pagan fertility rites. A considerable part of Sweden's land area lies within the Arctic circle and there the presence of the midnight sun is marked by a national holiday. Until a few generations ago it was the custom for Swedish swains to repair to springs in the forest on midsummer's night because they believed that to drink from them would give strength. On Midsummer's night Swedish girls are said still to sleep with seven different flowers under their pillows so that they may dream of their beloved.

This joyful celebration of the most fruitful season is a form of sun worship. It has long

Left: High summer does not seem to provide much sign of life or thaw as the Midnight Sun gleams over this chill, polar landscape. Yet this brief season is vital to the plant life of the Arctic and Antarctic.

been obvious to mankind that it is the strength and duration of the sun's rays that causes the buds to burgeon in the spring and the grain to ripen in the summer. These rays gain in intensity first in one hemisphere and then the other because of the angle at which the Earth's axis is tilted at the sun. The Earth spins on its axis, which runs through the Poles, once every 24 hours giving night and day. Besides this spinning, the Earth also revolves round the sun in a great elliptical orbit which it covers once a year. However, its axis is not absolutely perpendicular to the line of its orbit through space. If it were, the sun would be permanently over the equator and there would be no change of seasons. Because it is tilted 23.5 degrees from the perpendicular and the direction of its axis is absolutely fixed with respect to the stars, it follows that, at one point in its orbit, the northern hemisphere will be favoured by a 23.5 degree slant towards the sun. At exactly the opposite point on the yearly orbit the southern hemisphere will have the advantage of the full 23.5 degrees tilt towards the sun.

So long as our plant goes hurtling on its orbit through space the process continues. As each hemisphere is in turn presented at a more direct angle to the sun, it experiences a regular, annual rhythm of heating and cooling. This has its most marked effect in the more extreme latitudes where the angle towards the sun makes it more pronounced. The changing seasons follow one another in their order and, for a time each year, the Arctic and the Antarctic see the midnight sun. To those who live there it is a joyful and delightful day when, instead of sinking for a while below the horizon, the sun inscribes a circle round the sky.

The Eclipse of the Sun

The total eclipse of the sun by the moon is a grand and startling sight. All of us are used to the sun becoming obscured by cloud and, in England at least, very dim and gloomy days are not uncommon even at the height of summer. But the heaviest cloud covering does not have the ability to cut off the light as does the solid body of the moon. Experience of regular eclipses of the sun by the Earth (which we call nights) gives an idea of the pall of darkness that falls when the moon is between us and our star. The shock of this darkness is the greater because it is so sudden and so short-lived. When an eclipse takes place the dark shadow of the moon races across the ground towards the observer while an ever-growing black sphere bites into the golden disc of the sun. The darkness of the night falls suddenly just as the sun is completely masked. The black circle of the moon is haloed by the beautiful red corona of the sun and, in the right geographical location, the whole phenomenon can last for seven or eight minutes before the shadow moves on and normal daylight returns.

Something as dramatic and as rare as a total eclipse has naturally caused mass panic and other forms of unrestrained behaviour in the past when its cause has been imperfectly understood. Sun worship was common among both primitive and civilized societies. The reason for this was that all life on Earth depended on the heat and light of the sun – without it the world would spin through space a freezing, lifeless chunk of matter. Frequently an eclipse was seen by the ignorant as an attack on their god. The ancient Chinese were by no means ignorant and studied the movements of the heavenly bodies. They were under the impression, however, that an eclipse occurred when a

hungry dragon tried to swallow the sun. They attached great importance to thwarting the beast by making a lot of noise – banging drums, shouting, screaming and similar sorts of rowdy behaviour. The story goes that, in 2136 BC, the court astronomers failed to predict an eclipse and so the vital preparations were not made. Although the sun survived despite their inattention, the astronomers were executed – the ancient Chinese took a firm line with slackers. At one stage the ancient Romans considered it a legal offence and also in extremely bad taste even to suggest

Below: An eclipse photographed in Kenya.

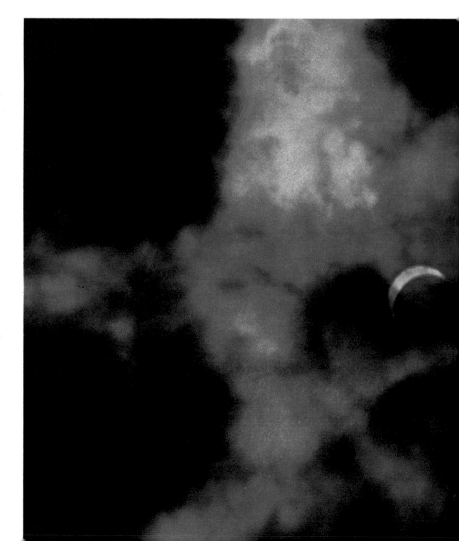

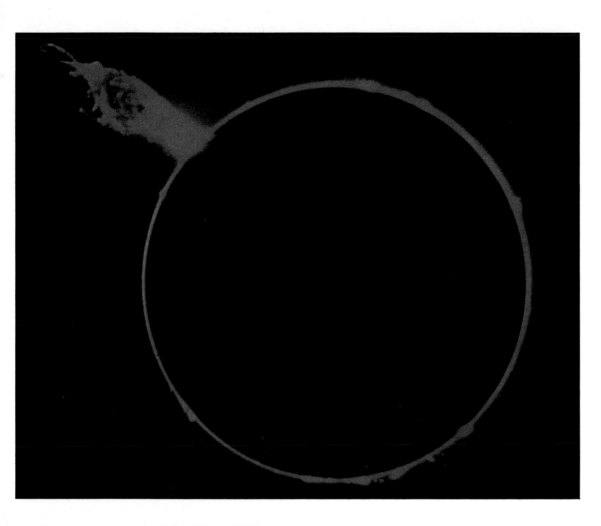

Left: The chromosphere (one of the sun's outer layers) and a prominence (a sheet of hot gas which flares out into space at great speed) are clearly visible in this photograph of an eclipse.

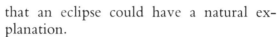

that an eclipse could have a natural explanation.

On a much later occasion Christopher Columbus exploited his knowledge of a lunar eclipse at a difficult stage of his voyages. On 2 April 1493 he threatened the inhabitants of Jamaica with a fearful divine vengeance if they did not supply the provisions which he needed desperately. He knew that a lunar eclipse was about to occur, and sure enough the Indians were so terrified by the eclipse that they begged him to bring back the moon and brought him his supplies. He overawed them by his apparent control of this terrifying event. Similarly, the ability to predict an eclipse was a powerful tool in the hands of astrologers who wielded their superior knowledge to great effect. Because the solar eclipse only lasts minutes the rituals devised by different cultures to bring back the sun appeared to work.

Columbus was a lucky man because a total eclipse is a very rare thing in any one place. For example, total eclipses have only been observable eight times from the British Isles since the fifteenth century and, on each occasion, only parts of the country have been favoured. The reason for this erratic performance is that the plane of the moon's orbit around the Earth does not coincide with the plane of the Earth's orbit around the sun. The two planes are at an angle of more than five degrees to one another so that when both moon and sun are up above, there is usually some apparent space between their bodies and, on the occasions when the moon is passing through a nodal point, which is where their apparent tracks intersect on the celestial sphere, the sun often is not. The seventeenth-century British astronomer Edmund Halley was the first to notice that an eclipse would occur every 18 years and 11.3 days at any one nodal point. This does not mean, however, that one particular eclipse will be recreated over the same spot every 18 years and 11.3 days because although Earth, moon and sun will be in the same relative positions, the Earth spins around once every 24 hours and so the eclipse will occur when it has spun 0.3 times further round than on the previous occasion. In other words the eclipse will be seen 120 degrees westward of its previous position.

The fact that a total eclipse happens at all is due to a number of remarkable coincidences. If the moon were smaller or the sun bigger, or if either of them were at different distances from the Earth, then the moon would not fit so snugly and exactly – its disc seems to be perfectly matched in size to that of the sun. This coincidence is only an apparent one, because the sun is millions of times the size of the moon but it is a lot further away. In fact, the moon does not prescribe a perfect circle around the Earth on its orbit and its path is elliptical. This means that it will sometimes be noticeably nearer to Earth than at other times when an eclipse occurs. When it is near to Earth it looms larger to us and a total eclipse can occur but, when it is farther away, it will have a bright solar ring when it is squarely in line with the target and this is called an annular eclipse.

Total eclipses are not only exciting spectacles, they also give astronomers a chance to observe the outer layers of the sun. The dark bulk of the moon cuts most of the dangerous glare and heat of the sun's bright photosphere and so makes possible direct observations of the outer chromosphere – an excitingly varied region in which vast red prominences and sudden luminous surges may occur which dwarf the Earth in size. Outside the chromosphere is the beautiful corona with its immense spiky streamers of sunlight. A number of interesting discoveries about the nature of the sun and the universe have been made by astronomers during the brief moments of an eclipse. Ideally, their observations are made from a high-altitude station so that the dust of the Earth's atmosphere does not detract from the clarity of vision. This means that, although suitable high places in the path of an eclipse are likely to be occupied by vast numbers of serious astronomers, it is well worth a journey, for those of us who are less committed, to watch such a remarkable event. The great speed with which the moon's shadow approaches and the sudden and surprising darkness (when the eclipse is complete there is less than half the light that is given by a full moon), together with the beauty of the sun's corona, make an eclipse a delightful and memorable experience.

Right: The Earth eclipsing the sun. The bright crescent above the Earth's surface is caused by the sun's light shining through the gases of the Earth's atmosphere. This photograph was taken from space by Apollo 12 astronauts.

The Eye of the Storm

The calm at the centre of a storm seems a far-fetched idea to those who have not experienced it. But there is an 'eye' to a hurricane, a hole of light cloud and warm, gentle winds, one-tenth the diameter of the total system with its terrifying prospect of towering banks of thick, black cloud above sheets of rain driven by howling winds. As the hurricane can be 480 kilometres (300 miles) across and travels at about 24 kmph (15 mph), the calm at its centre is merely a brief respite, a sign that half the storm has still to be faced. The eye is virtually walled in from the frenzied world outside by towering clouds which can reach up to 16 kilometres (10 miles) high.

The hurricane is a very tightly knit weather system which arises in the tropics from disturbances in the usually regular trade winds. Under certain circumstances a highly energetic heat engine will develop and this is a hurricane. Sea-water warmed by the sun will evaporate and by the process of convection and condensation will form thick clouds which will give extremely heavy rainfall. The evaporation and condensation of the water is the source of the energy of the storm. It takes about 600 calories of heat to produce the energy to evaporate one gram (0.03 ounces) of water and when this evaporated water is condensed into rain all the energy is released again, mostly in the form of heat but also (some three per cent of it) as kinetic energy. While it is over warm water, therefore, the hurricane is a sort of self-fuelling engine of destruction and it will only blow itself out when it loses the source of its fuel by passing over land or cold water. Even when it is deprived of energy in the shape of readily evaporating water by moving over land, it still holds enough to do a lot of damage before it runs down. Each storm varies in intensity but they all have considerably more energy than a million tons of TNT or a megaton thermonuclear weapon.

Although the hurricane is alone among weather systems in having an 'eye', its spiral shape (caused by the spinning of the Earth) is usual. As the warm moist air rises it creates low pressure (often as much as five per cent lower in the centre of the storm than at its periphery) and inflowing air rushes to replace it. When this inflowing air is travelling faster than 120 kmph (75 mph) it has reached hurricane force and has been known in some cases to exceed 240 kmph (150 mph). The strongest winds will be at the updraft in the centre of the system which will have assumed a spiral. This is because of the deflection caused by the spinning of the Earth, which sets up an anti-clockwise motion in low-pressure systems in the northern hemisphere (clockwise in the southern hemisphere). At the centre of the spiral and walled off by the shrieking winds will be the 'eye' of the storm.

Fortunately hurricanes are a rare phenomenon. The high winds and drenching rain can be destructive enough on their own account, particularly when the winds toss dangerous chunks of debris into the air, but they pose the greatest threat when the winds drive unusually high waves of sea-water before them. It is the flooding caused by the hurricane which takes the heaviest toll of human life. In November 1970 hurricane-driven floods caused the death of an estimated 300,000 people in Bangladesh – a natural disaster on a colossal scale. After this and other experiences there were attempts to seed embryo hurricanes with silver iodide

Above: An aerial view of the 'eye' at the centre of a hurricane shows that it is covered only in light, broken cloud in marked contrast to the dense cloud cover around it.

particles to encourage rainfall some distance from the 'eye' so that less energy would reach it to feed the storm. The problem is that any interference with the climate may have undesirable repercussions.

On a world-wide scale the most important task is to ensure that the information from satellites and radar is made use of in warning systems. High-risk areas would then be able to cope with hazardous conditions. Interestingly, hurricanes are usually given female names, and recently Australian women have objected to the idea that such a destructive and violent force should necessarily be considered female.

The forming of an 'eye' may be important not only to the development of a hurricane but to the more even distribution of temperature on the globe. The 'eye' is the vortex of the storm and it is there, or in the cloud wall around it, that almost all the work of transferring latent heat into kinetic energy takes place on condensation. But, as only three per cent of it is transferred into kinetic energy, the rest is released as heat which flows out and away from the upper end of the vortex. The chief beneficial effect of the currents of the global weather system is that they transport heat from the tropics, which receive too much of the sun's radiation, to the temperate zones which receive too little.

The 'eye' of the hurricane is more than a fascinating freak. It is a great deal more important than a strange, unexpected calm in the middle of a wild storm. In the crudest terms, it is a funnel of heat produced by the most dynamic and violent of weather systems and its existence may be one of the many vital factors which affect the environment we live in.

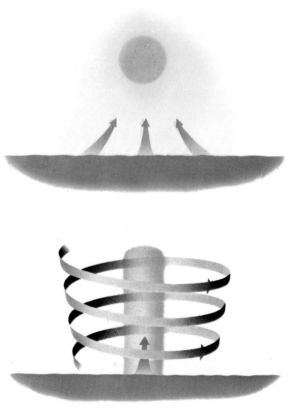

Left: The formation of a hurricane. Moist warm air rises as a columns from the warmed-up sea, disturbing the cold air it meets and creating a spiralling, corkscrewing wind. Several days elapse before this builds up into a hurricane-type wind. Until then it looks from above rather like a doughnut of cloud with its 'eye' as the hole in the centre.

Overleaf: This photograph of a hurricane from above illustrates perfectly the way in which clouds spiral out from its centre.

Lightning

Charred trees and shattered buildings all testify to the power of the lightning flash. A blow of such colossal force delivered from the threatening skies had only one explanation until recent times. It was believed that the thunderbolt was the special weapon of a powerful god. To the Greeks and Romans of the ancient world it was the unequalled missile of Zeus or Jupiter, the greatest in their pantheon of gods. In the mythology of the Norsemen it was the hammer blow of Thor, a god of immense strength who protected mankind from demons. Even in Christian times the damage done by a flash of lightning was often ascribed to God. The fact that tall buildings are in greater danger from lightning than lower ones often makes random strikes seem significant. Church spires and towers were among the tallest structures in the land and, when they were damaged, it seemed like God's judgment on the folly and pride of their builders or the sinfulness of their congregations.

In the eighteenth century, however, scientists began experiments with static electricity and it occurred to some that lightning might be electrical in origin. In 1752 Benjamin Franklin, American statesman and scientist, proved the point. He flew a kite in a thunderstorm, and he received an electric shock and a spark from a key attached to the bottom of the kite's string. It had therefore been proved that thunderstorms were electrically charged but certain mysteries remained. It takes such an enormous charge to pass a spark through even a few metres of air and, as lightning flashes can be photographed and measured eight kilometres (five miles) long, it was not clear how such a vast voltage could be built up.

Lightning is simply a huge spark, a dis-charge of several thousand amperes of current between the ground and the cloud. It has been computed that the driving force in an average flash of lightning is equal to that which can shift a 200 tonne train at 80 kmph (50 mph). This is not surprising as the air forms good insulation between the ground which is positively charged and the bottom of the cloud which is negatively charged. It is the vast numbers of raindrops present in the cloud which help to build up the enormous negative charge necessary to overcome the insulation of the intervening air. The drops are not all the same size and as they bounce off each other the large drops become negatively charged and accumulate at the bottom of the cloud while the small drops become positively charged and are swept to the top. As this happens millions of times in each cloud the charge builds up. Even so the resistance in a few metres of air can be too great for the increasing voltage to send a spark across. This is why high buildings, tall trees and mountain tops, which lessen the distance between Earth and cloud, are especially likely to be points from which the discharge takes place.

Distinction can be made between lightning that strikes downwards at trees, buildings or the ground, and 'sheet' lightning. The wind which blows the storm clouds along may change their shape and alter the distribution of the electrical charges within them. In this manner, a high charge may be built up on one side of the cloud so that the spark of lightning flashes from that side to the other within the cloud. Such strokes of lightning are splendidly reflected by the countless water droplets surrounding them and make a magnificent contribution to the spectacle that a thunderstorm provides.

Right: A jagged flash of lightning traces its crooked way along the line of least resistance. As air is more resistant to electricity than water, this line of least resistance is simply the wettest path from one point to another. Overleaf: Not all lightning strikes the ground. The strokes of 'sheet' lightning within clouds or from one cloud to another contribute to the spectacle and noise provided by an electrical storm.

These huge internal sparks, together with flashes from one cloud to another, are 'sheet' lightning and they are, of course, harmless except to people in flying machines. It is some consolation that 'sheet' lightning is much more common than flashes between clouds and the ground.

Lightning usually appears to be forked and jagged because the electrical charge is trying to find its easiest way to the ground. Air is a good insulator but water is not, so where there are more water droplets, more of the spark can be conducted on its way. The downward stroke of lightning is not the end of the matter because it is immediately followed by an upward return stroke which carries currents from the ground to the cloud. It is impossible to distinguish between the downward and return strokes with the naked eye because one follows the other in a fraction of a second and they both follow exactly the same path. This is because the downward stroke has ionized the channel of air through which it has travelled, and this ionized air is a particularly good conductor of electricity.

Although thunderstorms are a widespread and commonplace spectacle, they are uncanny and frightening. On average it is estimated that 360,000 lightning flashes occur every hour somewhere in the world. This should mean that we are accustomed to the phenomenon but this is not so. Humans can be extremely frightened during a storm, and cattle stampede and dogs crawl whimpering under beds.

This terror before lightning has long challenged man's myth-making ingenuity. In France and Germany it was believed that fires caused by lightning could only be extinguished by milk and elsewhere pregnant women and babies are believed to be immune to its effects. Cats and dogs are said to attract lightning as are certain species of trees such as the oak and the ash, 'beware of an oak: it draws the stroke; avoid the ash: it courts the flash'. In almost every culture lightning is associated with supernatural retribution. Although such beliefs no longer hold sway in our society, the superstition that lightning will never strike twice in the same place persists.

Etruscan soothsayers would work on the top of a high clear mountain, preferably above a grove of sacred oak trees. There they would observe the direction of lightning flashes exactly, taking note of their brilliance and where they appeared to strike. The soothsayers then calculated the incidence of danger and good fortune from each direction, and thus interpreted the omens for the person or city concerned.

It is not just the flashing lightning which causes such terror but the peals of thunder that accompany it at intervals. Thunder is simply the sound shock-wave produced when the air expands violently as it is heated by the electrical discharge. The interval between the flash and the sound occurs because light and sound travel at different speeds. We see the flash almost immediately, but sound takes roughly five seconds to cover 1.6 kilometres (one mile). The further away the lightning is, the greater the pause before the crash of thunder.

Even when one understands what causes it, a thunderstorm can be an exciting spectacle. The great tension which builds up between earth and sky never fails to awe and the power of the 'thunderbolt' commands our respect.

THE FERMENT BELOW

Our planet is not dead and unchanging. It is boiling and bursting with energy and life. Titanic forces are at work within the Earth and they steadily and continually change the appearance of the outer crust which seems so solid. Some of these changes are so slow that they are imperceptible: changes such as the building of mountain ranges, which may be growing at a rate of a metre a century, or the opening out of oceans such as the Atlantic, which did not exist 200 million years ago but which has been widening ever since at a rate of a few centimetres a year. Other changes are sudden and violent such as the volcanic action which raised Surtsey Island from the sea or the earthquakes which raze great cities. The power and the pressure which force the Earth's crust up, drag it down, fault it and split it are to be found deep beneath the surface in the still mysterious core and mantle of the globe.

Shock waves from earthquakes can travel through the whole body of the Earth and are recorded by seismographs placed all around the world. By recording the time these waves take to reach each seismograph from their common starting point at the earthquake's focus, scientists can gain some valuable information concerning the nature of the Earth's interior. If a seismograph is stationed only a few hundred kilometres away from a shock – just over the horizon – the waves which travel in a direct line between the two points only pass through a small section of the Earth. If the seismograph and shock are thousands of kilometres apart the waves go through a larger section and if they are on opposite sides of the world the waves have to go right through the middle. There are variations in the speed at which these waves travel and these variations are obviously due to the differences in the Earth's structure which they travel through. By very careful observation of this phenomenon and with the help of all possible sources of knowledge, scientists have composed a picture of the Earth's interior.

The density of the Earth's materials increases with depth and there are distinct boundaries between zones of different material. The innermost of the three major zones is the core. Evidence suggests that this is composed mostly of iron and nickel with a solid inner core and a liquid outer core. The iron-nickel meteorites which have been found provide indirect support for this theory. It is probably the liquid outer core that provides Earth with a magnetic field. As iron and nickel lose their magnetism at temperatures far lower than

Below: A glowing stream of lava gushes from Etna during its 1968 eruption. Volcanic products such as this are the principal materials for creating new land on the Earth's surface.

Previous page: Sakurajima is one of Japan's many active volcanoes. Immense forces are at work beneath the Earth's surface, producing side-effects which range from geysers to earthquakes.

those believed to exist in the core, the magnetic field is provided by a different mechanism. Convection currents cause eddies in the molten core and this swirling of liquid acts as a dynamo which puts out a magnetic field.

Outside the core is the thick rocky layer of the mantle. The composition of these rocks is presumably similar to that of those which have been discovered in stony meteorites. This would mean that they are made up largely from iron, magnesium and calcium silicates. The mantle is not absolutely solid and its texture varies from place to place. There is a subzone within the mantle which is called the asthenosphere and this is undoubtedly the one which has the most obvious and important effects upon the appearance of the surface and the world's environment. According to modern theory, earthquakes, volcanoes such as mighty Etna itself, mountains and continents have their origins in the movement of the asthenosphere. For, although this particular layer is not quite liquid, it is very plastic and can 'flow' or move slowly. Very slow convection currents through the asthenosphere cause the steady movement of everything above it – the outer mantle and the crust. These convection currents are the cause of plate tectonics – the movement of continents – which in turn are responsible for all the great earth movements from the raising of mountains to the opening out of oceans.

The outermost layer is very thin and composed of lighter rocks and this is known as the crust. The rocks of continents are granitic while those of the ocean floors are heavier and basaltic. The crust varies in thickness from 5 kilometres (3 miles) below some ocean floors to 70 kilometres (43 miles) beneath the highest parts of the continents. It seems that the crust is broken up into half-a-dozen major pieces or plates and a number of smaller ones. It is these plates which are shifted around by the currents from the asthenosphere and their clashing or tearing apart is the cause of so many natural phenomena and geological change. A world map of active volcanoes or of earthquake centres gives a remarkable picture of the lines along which some of these plates are pressing or dividing. The energies released by the vibrant interior of the Earth fold its exterior or erupt into the atmosphere. In their dying throes they produce such side-effects as geysers, lakes of sulphur and coloured crater pools. It is a poetic conceit that the Earth is in labour but it is not an inaccurate one.

Above: These volcanic cones in the Aleutian islands soar above the clouds in splendid, snow-capped symmetry. They appear to be twin volcanoes but are probably a parent volcano and its offspring. The creation of a volcanic cone can often seal up a vent which means that the magma finds a new vent at a point of weakness a short distance away and creates another volcanic cone in a later eruption.

Mount Etna

Above: A secondary vent on the side of Etna glows threateningly. Lava flows from secondary vents on this giant volcano have been known to extend for 24 kilometres (15 miles).

Etna, spewing rivers of fire down its massive sides and threatening to engulf villages with advancing heaps of smoking scoria, is an awe-inspiring example of a volcano's power. This 3,308 metre (10,855 feet) giant is the largest volcano in Europe and certainly one of the most active. Yet the whole, hulking, volcanic mountain is, by geologists' standards, a comparatively recent arrival on Earth and it is unlikely to maintain its present shape for long.

Mount Etna was born about 600,000 years ago when volcanic lava poured out from a fissure in the sea bed to form a cone at Calanna in Sicily. Over the centuries further cones formed or collapsed around the first in repeated eruptions. The highest cone, which formed a little to the west of the original one, was at Mongibello and that is the peak of present-day Etna. Although the whole volcano has been closely watched by scientists in modern times, not enough is known about it yet to predict when and how dangerously

or powerfully it will next erupt.

We do now know something of the titanic forces which are bottled up beneath the great mountain. The Earth, together with the other planets, probably began as a flaming ball of gas like the sun. During the immensely complex process of evolution, the Earth gradually cooled and its crust hardened. Far beneath this hard crust, which is still thickening, lies the molten core of the Earth. In addition, within the hardened crystal layers there are continually changing and reforming pockets of molten silicates in which varying amounts of gas are dissolved. This is the material which simmers beneath all volcanoes and it is known as magma. A volcano is simply a weak spot where magma breaks up to the surface. When this happens the gas begins to rise through the magma as bubbles do in a bottle of soda-water when the top is taken off. At this stage the volcano is erupting and a number of different things – all more or less impressive and terrifying – may occur. The ferocity of the eruption depends on the amount of gas in the magma, the sort of pressures on it, whether it is sticky or very liquid and how big or small the escape fissure is. No two volcanoes and indeed no two eruptions of one volcano are the same.

At the height of their activity volcanoes seem to be alive and the most graphic myths abound to explain their terrifying animation. The primitive peoples of Chile, for instance, believed that a fearsome whale lived inside volcanoes, while the ancient Japanese imagined a great spider lurking in the bowels of the earth. In Indonesia it was the terrible snake, Hontobogo by name, which held up the whole world with its writhing body; but

when Hontobogo was restless and moved, the whole Earth shook, fire shot out of the mountains and even the powerful gods were dismayed. The Roman god of fire, Vulcan, gave his name to volcanoes and he was depicted swearing and sweating as he worked in his great forge under the volcanoes, making weapons for the other gods and forging Jove's thunderbolts.

The early Romans and Greeks were very impressed both with the fertility of Etna's slopes and her periodic eruptions. Etna was believed to have been the result of Jove's initial struggle with the giants or Titans who resisted the attempts of the Olympian gods to change the laws of heaven. Jove in his exasperation unleashed the winds and waters against them and so they were defeated and crushed beneath the tumbling mountains. In one version of the legend Jove flung Etna on top of the giant Typhon and so when Etna erupted, he was making frantic attempts to escape from his smouldering prison.

The oldest record of a volcanic eruption relates to Mount Etna herself. The great poet Pindar, who lived in the fifth century BC wrote an ode describing the contest between the gods and the giants. His work is given great force because he drew upon accounts of Etna's behaviour to describe the events, and experts now believe that his graphic detail was probably derived from the eruptions of Etna in 479 BC. He described Etna in Sicily as 'the pillar of the sky' from which fire spewed with a resounding roar. By day burning streams of lava poured down the sides of the mountain into the wide valleys while at night white-hot blocks of stone crashed into the woods, setting fire to them, and then rolled into the sea where they sank down to the bottom.

Etna has always possessed the ability to surprise and to cause damage. In AD 122, an

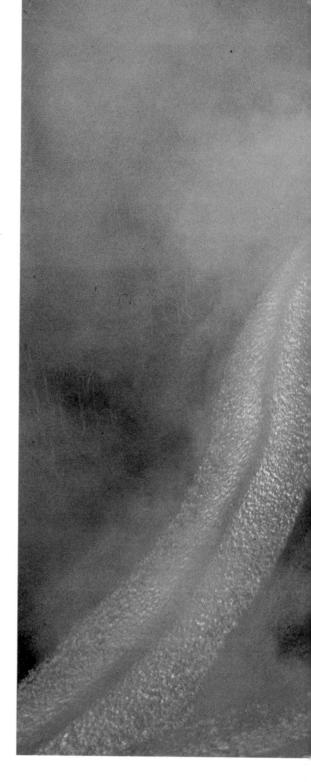

eruption from Etna destroyed the town of Catania. In 1381 the port of Ulisse was made useless when lava from the mountain filled in the harbour. In 1669 the people of Catania attempted to divert an anticipated lava stream from the city by protecting themselves with animal hides and a rampart. But their enterprise was quashed by the villagers of Paterno who realized that the lava was directed towards their fields and homes, and Catania with some of the surrounding villages was once again badly damaged. The Catanians were confronted with an ever-present dilemma; it is useless to divert a lava flow unless it can be directed towards uncultivated and uninhabited land.

There have been numerous, less damaging eruptions and in 1974 the destructive fury of the mountain was captured on television film. The film showed streams of molten lava, composed of magma, spewing from the mountain, setting alight the undergrowth on Etna's flanks. It also showed villagers praying that their houses and fields would be saved from the glowing, advancing mounds of ash and scoria made up from the magma which had been hurled into the air by explosions within the mountain and cooled into solid but burning drops looking like clinker. Sicilians have always prayed for relief from Etna's fury. In classical times worshippers of the goddess Ceres gathered on her slopes, in the thirteenth century the Catanians carried the veil of St Agatha in fervent procession, and today the saints are still patiently invoked for divine mercy.

Yet Etna is a comparatively gentle giant and its eruptions are mild. This is because the magma under Etna is more fluid and less sticky than it is under some other volcanoes so that trapped gases can escape from it more easily. Where the lava is so sticky as to be almost solid the gases can only burst out with explosive force. Such explosions have caused some of the most cataclysmic disasters on record. The mighty explosion of Krakatoa, for example, dwarfed that of any atom bomb. Krakatoa was a group of three volcanic cones which formed two uninhabited islands in the Sunda Strait between Java and Sumatra. In May 1883 the first cone began to throw out

ash and pumice. In June and August the other cones began to erupt. This activity reached its colossal climax on 26 and 27 August when, in a series of shattering explosions, two of the volcano's cones completely destroyed themselves and the third split in half. These massive blasts were heard 4,828 kilometres (3,000 miles) away and fragments of various sorts were hurled many kilometres into the air. There was a heavy rain of pumice and ash and the dust did not settle until the following year. This rain was so thick over Sumatra that it blotted out the light and kept the skies dark for two days. But the really catastrophic effects of the explosions came from the tidal waves which they caused and which crashed down on the thickly-populated islands of Java and Sumatra. The greatest tidal wave was 39 metres (130 feet) high in places and, because of it and others, over 36,000 people were killed.

There is a long history of volcanic erup-

Above: Smouldering lava flows down Etna's slopes. Such lava streams destroy farmland in their paths – although ultimately they will create fertile new land.

tions which have caused dreadful disasters. The most famous is the eruption of Vesuvius in AD 79 which suddenly overwhelmed the town of Pompeii with a rain of hot ash and stifling gases leaving it and its slaughtered inhabitants as in a time capsule, perfectly preserved beneath the lava for archaeologists of later generations. Much later, in 1902, a glowing cloud was blasted from the vent of Mont Pelée on Martinique in the West Indies. This cloud was composed of ash-laden gases which, loaded with debris from the explosion, hurtled down on the town of St Pierre and razed it, killing its population of 30,000 within minutes.

Such violence and such a toll of human life would make volcanoes seem to be a dreadful natural scourge. However impressive their eruptions and however awesome their power, it would seem that people should live as far away from such unpredictable neighbours as possible. It seems strange that humans should cluster on Mount Etna farming the dangerous slopes. However, volcanoes offer rewards as great as perils. They create new land – most of the Earth's islands are volcanic in origin – and most of that land is extremely fertile. Volcanic ash contains precious fertilizers such as potassium and phosphorus.

Besides, volcanism is part of the essential process of evolution which the Earth is undergoing The recent exploration of the moon has shown that this process is not confined to Earth and that volcanism may be part of evolution throughout the universe. There is a theory that life itself originated from volcanic matter. So mighty Etna is not just an awesome and dangerous natural freak but one of the greatest marvels in nature and a vital part of all creation.

Left: Vesuvius, Italy's other great volcano, erupted in AD 79, destroying Pompeii and Herculaneum. It then collapsed inwards to form a huge caldera. The outer edge of this can be seen in the background. In the foreground is the crater of the new volcanic structure which has grown up within the caldera.

The Pools of Keli Mutu

Keli Mutu is a volcano with three differently coloured crater lakes. These bright pools of green or red are only a few metres apart on the huge flanks of a giant shield volcano. Keli Mutu itself is one of many volcanoes in the famous 'ring of fire' which surrounds the Pacific. It stands among 50 others on the island of Flores which is the second largest of the lesser Sunda islands in Indonesia. The pools lie in closely grouped craters on its crown, relics of the last eruption in the 1860s. The romantically named Tiwoe Ata Polo (Lake of the Bewitched People) is a dark and striking red. Close beside it is the Tiwoe Noea Moeri Kooh Fai (Lake of the Young Men and Virgins) on the shores of which a smoking volcanic solfatara (vent) gives warning of the mountain's activity while its waters gleam an opaque green. The last lake, Tiwoe Ata Mboepoe, is also green, but its waters are clear and transparent and therefore markedly different from those of its muddy neighbour. The magic colours of these strange pools have always excited curiosity – why do three crater lakes so close to one another look so different?

By a strange trick the chemical and mineral content of each lake is different. The red Lake of the Bewitched People contains a large amount of iron salts in solution and that tends to produce a 'Coca Cola' colour just as it does in the famous 'Black' tributaries of the Amazon river. The green Lake of the Young Men and Virgins holds free sulphuric and hydrochloric acids as does the Tiwoe Ata Mboepoe which has less sediment in its clearer waters.

Taken individually the coloured lakes are not surprising. Green lakes occur on other volcanoes as a result of exactly the same corrosive addition of sulphuric and hydroch-

loric acids to their waters. The solfatara that can be observed by the waters of the Lake of the Young Men and Virgins is the clue to the origin of the acid. The solfatara is a small orifice in the mountain which emits gases as a result of minor volcanic activity. Hydrogen sulphide and hydrochloric acid vapour are among the principal gases given off by volcanoes as they bubble out of the magma which is the seething heart of all volcanic action. So the hydrochloric acid is already there and the hydrogen sulphide rapidly becomes oxidized as it steams from the mountain and makes contact with the air. Once oxidized, it turns into sulphuric acid. The red lake is slightly less common than the green ones. Magma is principally a silicate melt which commonly includes iron. When magma reaches the surface during an eruption it cools and solidifies to form volcanic rocks and evidently the rocks which cooled around the basin of the Lake of the Bewitched People happened to be rich in easily oxidized iron from the original magma.

It is strange to find such diverse conditions on the same mountain, but the presence of solfataras and the resultant circulation of gases within the mountain lead in this instance to the production of minerals by a process called pneumatolytic differentiation. This is when bubbles of gas are forced up through the magma and carry with them substances, such as iron, sodium, titanium and phosphorus with strong affinities to the gases. These substances are dissolved into the gas under tremendous pressure deep down in the magma and then rise towards the surface.

This process of differentiation may have led to a greater concentration of easily oxidized iron at the red lake but it is more

Above: Tiwoe Ata Polo (Lake of the Bewitched People) which at its most startling is a dark and variable red, with the green Tiwoe Noea Moeri Kooh Fai (Lake of the Young Men and Virgins) in the background.

likely that it has had an effect on the corrosive ability of the acidic water. There are numerous chemical changes that might occur owing to the presence of some element in the crater of this lake which is not found in the other two – the presence of copper, for instance, would kill off all algae which would change the chemical character of the water. It is probable that there is some element found in the bed of the Lake of the Bewitched People which gives its acidic water an increased ability to corrode iron and thus build up a heavy iron content and a dark red colour.

The root cause in the difference in colour between lakes is that the distribution of silicates within the magma below Keli Mutu became very uneven owing to pneumatolytic differentiation. When an eruption occurred the contents of the rocks which hardened from the overflowing magma melt varied from place to place. The Lake of the Bewitched People came to be rich in iron either because the rock in its bed held an unusually high quantity of iron silicates or because it held traces of some element which increased the corrosive power of its acidic waters. The strange colouring of the pools is due to chemical changes deep in the heart of the mountain which they crown. The deep red and the brilliant green are vivid and eye-catching and they provide a sensational and surprising contrast with one another.

Old Faithful Geyser

Old Faithful must be the world's best known geyser. When it erupts it spits 45,460 litres (10,000 gallons) of water to a height of between 30 and 45 metres (100 and 150 feet) in the air in a remarkable display of powerful subterranean forces. The intriguing thing about Old Faithful is the way that the timing of its eruptions hardly varies. Every discharge lasts for five minutes and then the geyser is quiet for about one hour, give or take 20 minutes, until groaning and rumblings herald a jet of steam followed by the next eruption of a column of water which is heated to more than 100°C (212°F). Old Faithful's scalding water runs into the aptly named Firehole River in America's Yellowstone National Park, a natural playground of volcanic marvels.

It was because of its punctuality that the geyser was given its name by General Henry D. Washburn who discovered it in 1870. Since then over 25,000 of its eruptions have been recorded in the last 85 years and they have hardly varied. Indeed, the American

Right: One of the regular eruptions of Old Faithful in Yellowstone National Park, Wyoming. Over 25,000 such eruptions have been recorded within the past 85 years.
Below right: How a geyser works. Water is heated by very hot volcanic rocks, deep below the surface. It becomes hot enough to boil at a point in the geyser's tube which causes water and steam to gush out at the top. Once the geyser's tube is empty, it gradually refills with cold water and the process is repeated.

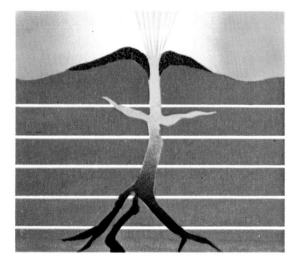

Indians claim that Old Faithful was gushing away regularly long before the first white man appeared on the scene.

This steaming blowhole is not a unique phenomenon. It has plenty of competition within Yellowstone Park itself where there are over 100 true geysers and numerous hot springs. One of the geysers, known as the Giantess, is bigger than Old Faithful and throws a jet 76 metres (250 feet) into the air. The biggest geyser ever seen was the Waimangu which appeared in New Zealand at the beginning of the century. But the Waimangu faded away after five years when the level of nearby Lake Tarawere fell after the collapse of a natural dam, an incident which must have subtly affected the underground pressures which make a geyser.

Geysers are minor forms of volcanism and are found in volcanic areas. The three areas in which they are most plentiful are Taupo in New Zealand, Yellowstone National Park in the United States and Iceland. The word geyser comes from the Icelandic *geysir* meaning a gusher or rager and the original Great Geysir is in Iceland. Other geysers can be found in Japan, Java, Sumatra, the Celebes and the Aleutians. None of them is as predictably spectacular as Old Faithful – the Great Geysir in Iceland erupted every 30 minutes in 1772 but, by 1883, only spouted every 20 days.

The regularity of eruptions is the result of a number of variable factors. At the bottom of every geyser is a fissure or chamber of very hot water vapour and gas. Above this is a pipe to the surface and the sides of this pipe may well have been smoothed and strengthened by mineral deposits carried in the geyser's water. At the beginning of the geyser's activity, the pipe will be full of

Far left: Old Faithful in action. The geyser has been called 'faithful' because of the constant interval between its eruptions – about 67 minutes each time.
Left: Intriguing rock shapes add charm to Yellowstone Park's 'grotto' geyser. It erupts several times a day and sends a jet of water up to 10 metres (33 feet) high.

comparatively cool groundwater which will be constantly heated and pressured by the super-heated steam in the chamber below it. The moment of eruption occurs when the groundwater lower down the pipe turns to steam, expands, pushes the rest of the water out of the pipe in a jet and clears the way for some of the steam and gas to escape. When all this has happened, the pressure from the chamber is relieved and groundwater will be able to fill up the pipe again, ready to be blasted up in another scalding fountain when the steam below reaches the critical pressure.

All of the heat and some of the hot water and steam of geysers and hot springs are generally of volcanic origin, but there is commonly a proportion of surface-derived groundwater mixed in at the most productive geysers. As molten matter beneath the Earth's surface cools and solidifies, it gives off steam and carbon dioxide which finds its way up through cracks and fissures in the Earth and gradually cools down as it heats up the rocks that it passes through. If this

steam is still hot enough when it reaches the surface and if it finds a tailor-made fissure or pipe, it will form a geyser.

Not all hot springs occur in volcanic areas. Some of the luxurious health resorts which make up Europe's spas are sited on thermal waters caused by different means. Sometimes water, circulating deep underground, comes into contact with very hot, but not volcanic, rocks and then rises by convection to the surface. At other times, and more rarely, water can be heated by a chemical reaction; water passing through anhydrous calcium sulphate deposits, for example, would turn them into gypsum but this chemical transformation would give off intense heat.

Geysers usually occur in volcanic areas. Old Faithful's home in Yellowstone Park, thousands of metres up in the Rocky Mountains, is on a plateau of volcanic rock underlain by pockets of rock which are still hot. Up there the world's best known geyser hurls a great wall of water into the air with the steady regularity of a giant pulse.

The Island of Surtsey

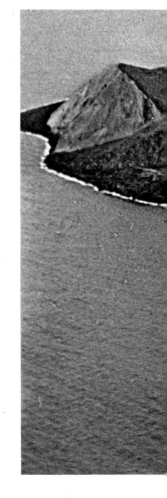

In just under three years a completely new island was blasted up from the sea bed near Iceland to find a place on the geographers' maps. The whole spectacular firework display was the result of volcanic action beneath the sea bed. The island was named Surtsey or the island of Surt. Surt was the giant who, according to Nordic mythology, will set the world on fire in a grim finale when the twilight of the gods descends.

Surtsey first served notice of its appearance with a series of explosions beginning at 8 a.m. on 14 November 1963. These occurred about nine kilometres (six miles) south west of Iceland where the sea was 122 metres (400 feet) deep. Naturally explosions from such a depth produce great jets and columns of steam but these were loaded with more solid volcanic matter such as scoria, ash and blocks of cooled lava. Later in the day, dark jets of vapour laden with matter reached 152 metres (500 feet) into the air while columns of steam towered 3,000 metres (10,000 feet) above. By 16 November the mound of scoria and lava pieces had grown so that something which looked like an island of clinker began to emerge from the sea. By this stage Surtsey was 500 metres (1,640 feet)

Left: The eruptions which created Surtsey. The clouds of gas and steam which hang over the emerging island are dark with scoria and volcanic ash.

long and 39 metres (130 feet) above sea-level.

Although the island had appeared, there was at that stage no reason to expect it to survive for long. Despite the fact that most of the world's islands are of volcanic origin, the process which was building Surtsey was peculiarly threatened with erosion by the seas. Unlike more permanent islands formed of solidified lava which is first emitted in a liquid form, Surtsey was no more than a heap of volcanic fragments. Rather than being one armoured mass, the island resembled a pile of clinker and the sea was eroding it all the time. A similar island had appeared to the South of Sicily in 1831 and caused much political excitement as it was instantly claimed by the British, French, Neapolitans and Spaniards. The political excitement soon died down when Graham Island (or Hotham or Ferdinandea or Corrao as it was variously named by its would-be owners) was swallowed up by the sea. A similar fate seemed about to befall Surtsey – even the original farce seemed certain to be re-enacted as two enterprising French journalists landed

on the island between eruptions to hoist the tricolour.

The new island began to gain the chance of greater permanence, however, when it developed in a different manner. It had, at first, appeared only around part of the underwater crater which was hurling up all the debris. But, by April 1964, the scoria had grown into a cone which completely surrounded the crater and protected it from sea-water. The volcano was then able to spew out liquid lava to bond together the scoria. The flow of lava lasted with periods of greater and lesser intensity until 7 May 1965. A fortnight later another eruption began to the north east of Surtsey, and by September a smaller island appeared. This new piece of land soon vanished as a result of the sea's erosion showing how narrowly the first island had escaped such a fate.

It is not surprising that Surtsey appeared in the vicinity of Iceland. The whole area lies across a mid-ocean ridge which marks the divide between two tectonic plates. These plates – huge, rigid sections of the Earth's

Right: A huge column of gas and smoke issues from the newly arrived island that was to become Surtsey.

crust – are continuously moving about upon convection flows which rise through the Earth's mantle. The American plate is tearing away from the European plate in mid-Atlantic at the rate of a few centimetres a year and, where the plates move apart, volcanic material wells up and spreads over the ocean floor. Iceland is the world's largest single piece of land entirely of volcanic origin and is surrounded by islands like Surtsey which have suddenly appeared from the sea.

Volcanoes have always been creators of new land, and the continual volcanic activity in and around Iceland is of immense scientific interest. Fumaroles, geysers and hot springs are common throughout Iceland and the frequent eruptions of the volcanoes Katla and Grímsvötn, which lie beneath glaciers, cause the ice to melt resulting in flooding. Iceland was believed to be the mysterious land of Thule which features in Nordic mythology as a fiery island, a place of punishment in one legend. Surt's role in the twilight of the gods was to lead an avenging band of fire giants: lightning flashed from his sword and all around him flames sprang from the cracking Earth.

The final act thus far in the birth of Surtsey occurred in August 1966. A new and plentiful flow of lava began on the island giving it a harder 'crust' to withstand the sea. So, unless there is further far-reaching volcanic action on the site, the maps of the world have gained a new island. Certain species of wild life have readily accepted Surtsey as a haven: seals have been seen dozing on its warm beaches and numerous sea birds have settled on it.

172

The Sulphur Pools
of Yellowstone

Gleaming upon the water and crusting the rocks in parts of America's fabulous Yellowstone National Park is the unmistakable yellow of sulphur. It is not just the colour but the memorable, nostril-clearing fumes of sulphur which steam up from certain pools that are eloquent testimony to its presence. It is not a particularly lovely aspect of one of the world's most fantastic volcanic playgrounds but it is certainly an interesting one. It comes as a mild surprise to see sturdy trees and healthy grasses growing close to waters that, at their most charmless, look like effluent from a chemical factory. Yet the strange, yellowish water adds to the exotic appeal of the Park which boasts bubbling cauldrons of mud, 200 geysers and 3,000 hot springs. The reek of unexpected gases in the air gives a feeling of excitement, a feeling that one is in a natural theatre which will present a show of unusual sights and unmask a display of seething activity. The sulphur pools are part of a parade of the minor effects of volcanism.

To the superstitious sulphur has been the incontrovertible smell of hell up to recent times. Whenever the devil appeared he always left behind him a scent of sulphur, or so our ancestors believed as they sniffed cautiously about the abode of some wretched crone suspected of witchcraft. The medieval technique of scientific deduction was not above reproach but there were in fact reasons for associating sulphur with hell. Among the scholars of an earlier age the real existence of hell was undisputed and its geographical location was 'down below' or somewhere beneath the Earth. Sulphur generally appears naturally as a product of volcanic action and so it seems to issue from the bowels of the Earth out of steaming vents such as solfataras, all of which added, incidentally, to the belief that hell was uncomfortably hot. Numerous early descriptions of hell feature steaming and scorching lakes of fire and brimstone; hell is described as an abyss of flame, a huge furnace or oven. The souls there live in fire as fish live in water, but it is inside them as well as outside. They breathe it and their blood boils in their veins, and their hearts, brains and entrails seethe and simmer. The fire is the blaze of God's wrath which in the Old Testament consumes sinners like rubbish. In the Apocalypse Satan is thrown into a lake of fire and brimstone and so any emissary from Satan's kingdom was sure to trail a sulphurous smell. As late as the mid-nineteenth century hell was still associated with volcanic action and it was argued that its torments were to be found at the centre of the earth, the source of all fiery volcanic eruptions. But sulphur pools, fumes, boiling mud and steaming jets of water fail to make Yellowstone a hellish place. The sulphur is more fascinating than sinister. It is one of the special effects of an area that is most truly described as a volcanic playground.

Despite the fact that it is one of the most prominent products of volcanism, sulphur is not one of the most common elements in the Earth's crust. Indeed, it forms only a fraction of one per cent of the crust's composition but seems nevertheless to be given prominence in volcanic action. As far as can be ascertained, sulphur dioxide and hydrogen sulphide are among the seven or eight principal gases to be given off by volcanoes. The list of volcanic gases may not be complete because scientific observation of exploding volcanoes and their emissions is obviously very dangerous. Enough is

known, however, to state that sulphurous fumes are given off from a significant number of volcanoes. As far as thermal springs are concerned – and these are mostly the result of heating from volcanic rocks far below the surface – they are either acidic or rich in hydrogen sulphide which makes them sulphurous.

Considerable volcanic forces were active in the Yellowstone Park area 60,000 years ago and still labour away far below the surface. Indeed, the National Park is situated on a rhyolite plateau and, as rhyolite is generally the produce of violent and explosive eruptions, the area must have been much less agreeable at its most active. There are still hot rocks below the plateau and when surface water moves down through cracks in the surface it becomes heated by contact with them and resurfaces as steam. In addition to this, molten material far beneath gives off volatile substances as it cools, mainly in the form of water vapour, which can be associated with hydrogen sulphide. So traces of sulphur are common

in the heated water which gushes out all over Yellowstone Park and it even encrusts dry vents where activity has temporarily ceased.

One of the main values of Yellowstone National Park, apart from the spectacular features of volcanic activity, is that it preserves within itself not only the natural countryside but also its threatened animal species. Scientific research which would be impossible outside a controlled environment is made possible and the area is a delight to visitors. Yogi Bear is probably the most well-known fictional inhabitant of Yellowstone or 'Jellystone' but the park does protect animals such as the American black bear and the American bison or buffalo. By 1890 due to perverse and systematic slaughter by the white settlers it looked as if the buffalo was doomed to extinction until its survival was entrusted to the newly opened national parks and the 835 remaining head were saved.

In the late nineteenth century in America concern was expressed by early conservationists about the dangers to the natural environments posed by the gigantic expan-

Above: Encrustations of sulphur around vents such as this one at Pozzuoli in Italy gave them the name of solfataras from 'solfo' which is Italian for sulphur.

Left: Sulphur springs at Dallol, Lake Karum in Ethiopia.

sion of private property as the frontiers were pushed westwards. In the collective rush towards the Pacific many people managed to make themselves the owners of such large personal 'parks' that it was feared there would be no free land for others seeking green space in which to relax. The supporters of the reservation of parts of Yellowstone were helped by a report published in 1865 on the superb Yosemite Valley in California: 'unless means are taken by government to withhold them from the grasp of individuals, all places favourable in scenery to recreation of the mind and body, will be closed against the great body of the people'.

The first white man to discover Yellowstone was John Colter whose objectives were simply to find good beaver country and to observe Indian movements. During the winter of 1807 he set out on a solo exploration and discovered such wonders as hot springs, boiling mud-holes and geysers. People did not believe stories of 'Colter's Hell' and thought his account of the exotic place to be totally preposterous. In the 1870s, however, a respectable surveyor, Ferdinand Hayden, confirmed Colter's earlier testimony although he claimed primacy for the discovery of Yellowstone's natural marvels. 'The beholder stands amazed at nature's handiwork', he noted.

The plateau had such an effect upon its first white visitors and conveyed such an impression as to its value and uniqueness that they determined to preserve it from exploitation. The area was kept from private ownership as a pleasure-ground for all the citizens of the nation by a ruling of Congress in 1872. This made Yellowstone the first ever national sanctuary.

Earthquakes

Sometimes it sounds like the roar of an approaching express train. The lights sway and the church bells ring while buildings crack and collapse into rubble. The ground vibrates, heaves, buckles and even cracks open in gaping fissures where the earth is soft. These are some of the effects of an earthquake – a terrifying demonstration of forces far beyond the control of man.

It is difficult to choose the worst earthquake in history, but the 1923 tremor which almost destroyed Tokyo and Yokohama, killing 143,000 people, was one of the most destructive. Lisbon in 1755 and San Francisco in 1906 suffered annihilating experiences. The 1964 quake in Alaska was, geologically, one of the most violent ever recorded but, due to the sparsity of population in that region, the cost in terms of life and property was comparatively mild. The effects of this monstrous Alaskan tremor were so widespread, however, that swimming pools sloshed about in an unnerving manner as far away as Texas. It now seems likely that the worst disaster occurred in the dreadful upheaval in Tang-shan in eastern China in 1976. Owing to the nature of the Chinese regime full details of the tragedy have not yet emerged and perhaps never will. A death toll of 655,000 has been claimed and this seems likely to be accurate. It is a sobering thought that, with so many cities located in dangerous areas, it is only a matter of time before this gruesome record is broken.

These earthquake-prone areas are easily discovered by plotting on a world map all the foci or origins of historically recorded quakes. They fall into a clearly marked series of narrow belts. The circum-Pacific Belt holds many prominent names on the list of shattered cities and countries – San Francisco, Guatemala City, Huarás in Peru, the Philippines, Tokyo, and Anchorage in Alaska. The second great earthquake belt is the Himalaya–Mediterranean Belt in which Friuli in Italy, Gediz and Lice in Turkey and Quetta in Pakistan, among others, have been devastated. The Northern China Belt, which was responsible for the Tang-shan quake, together with various lesser known ones, completes the zones which mark the boundaries of the dozen or so great plates into which the Earth's crust is broken. These plates of almost rigid rock form a shell around the more plastic inner zones of the Earth, and very slow convection currents rising from the Earth's molten core mean that the plates are slowly but continually grinding against one another. The movements along these plate boundaries are the source of the earthquake's destructive power. The worst shocks are caused where one plate slowly rides over another, which makes Japan a peculiarly ill-placed country as it marks the line on which the Asian plate is riding over the Pacific Ocean plate. Destructive quakes are also caused where two plates grind sideways past each other as they do along the famous San Andreas fault in California. Here the American plate is moving northwards while its neighbouring Pacific plate edge is, relatively speaking, either holding steady or moving southwards. Earthquakes are less violent where two plates are moving apart. When this happens volcanoes develop and molten rock pours up through the widening fracture. The places where plates are pulling away from each other are usually in mid-ocean, but Iceland sits on one such spot. As a result Iceland is the site of great seismic and volcanic activity and the famous beauty spot of

Above: A section of the San Andreas fault in California where two plates grind sideways against each other. This fault caused the disastrous earthquake of San Francisco in 1906.

Thingvellir, the country's ancient legislative centre, is surrounded by volcanoes and fractures which can cause earthquakes.

The great rock movements which cause quakes very rarely leave a mark on the Earth's surface. This is because the earthquake may take place at anything up to 80 kilometres (50 miles) below ground level. The beginnings of the disturbance occur when stresses build up in the rock on a plate boundary or individual fault. Rock is not always the solid, toe-stubbing substance it seems but is plastic at certain depths beneath the Earth's surface. The pressure of the blocks of rock stressed against each other on either side of a fault causes them to bend because the friction between them is too great to allow them to slide smoothly past one another. Eventually the strain within the rock overcomes the friction on the fault and the rock masses snap back to an unstrained position with a jerk. This jerk sets up great shockwaves and these are what is known as an earthquake. In solid rocks the actual movement can rarely be seen even though the vibration is enough to shatter buildings or to set water swaying into enormous waves. Some of these waves are big enough to cross oceans and are popularly, but wrongly, called tidal waves: seismologists prefer to call them by their Japanese name of tsunami. Other dramatic effects of earthquakes are great fissures, capable of swallowing people and animals, which open in the ground when soft sediments slide and settle.

In some cases the rock movements that cause a quake do leave a scar on the surface. During the great San Francisco earthquake of 1906, a house on California's San Andreas fault was shifted sideways along its garden for more than 6 metres (21 feet) so that the front path led to the living-room window rather than the door. Throughout the upheaval, the timber frame building remained intact, hardly affected by the vibrations. A few kilometres away it was a different story – the concrete buildings of San Francisco shattered and sank into their sediment foundations. In less than a minute a great city died.

The Giant's Causeway

The Giant's Causeway off the Antrim coast of Ireland is a dramatic example of unexpected symmetry in nature. So regular are its black basalt columns that they were long thought to be the work of stonemasons pursuing some grandiose but obscure purpose. The Causeway itself appears as a mass of closely stacked columns – more than 32,000 of them – extending some 183 metres (600 feet) out to sea. At the end of this strange pier the basalt disappears beneath the waves and inland it is lost beneath cliffs of other rocks so that the total number of columns is not known. Their average diameter is about 45 centimetres (18 inches) and most of them form hexagons in cross-section although there are plenty of pentagons, heptagons and other geometric shapes. Most of the columns are more than 9 metres (30 feet) long although few of such length are visible in the Causeway. On the cliffs above, similarly shaped sticks of basalt can be seen in section so that they decorate the cliffside making it look like a loft of rather angular organ pipes.

The Irish myth holds that the natural structure was the beginning of a bridge or causeway that giants had once tried to build between Ireland and Scotland. The most repeated tale is that the Causeway was laid down by the giant and epic warrior Finn MacCoul who had invited the Scottish colossus Benandonner over for a fight and wished to spare him wet feet before the contest. Such legends are commonly attached to blocks of stone which occur naturally and appear to be strewn about by giants in some prehistoric game. According to another typical story from Dorset, the local Giant's Grave was caused by two giants in contest. They both stood on a hill and hurled rocks but the one whose rock fell shortest was so mortified that he died of vexation, thus irrevocably shaping the landscape. Sometimes even man-made megalithic remains have been popularly attributed to the giants of yore.

The truth behind the Giant's Causeway is barely less spectacular than the romance. Fifty million years ago Antrim was in the heart of a great volcanic region which also embraced the western islands of Scotland, Iceland and the east coast of Greenland. These countries were then closer together than they are now; the reason for the volcanic activity was the opening up of the northern Atlantic Ocean as North America and Eurasia tore steadily apart. This widening of the ocean still continues today, but only Iceland is now in the active zone. Where great segments or plates of the Earth's crust move apart, molten rock (volcanic magma) pours up through the opening fissures between them. In Antrim the sheets of liquid lava spread out over the area and started to solidify as they cooled down. While they were cooling they contracted a little so that shrinkage fractures formed – just as they do in the sun-dried mud of a harbour at low tide. The consistency of cooling lava is such that it will tend to form straight shrinkage cracks and, if the pattern of cooling is regular enough, these will form a network of hexagons. As the lava cooled through its depth the hexagonal surface cracks extended downwards and formed the edges of the massive columns visible today. Thousands of years of erosion have followed the formation of the columns and they have worn the Antrim coast down until one spectacular, jointed lava flow – the Giant's Causeway – now stands upon the beach.

Right: The famous basalt columns of the Giant's Causeway. Although weathering has rounded and smoothed most of the exposed edges of stone, the pillars on the left still look clear-cut as though shaped by a mason.

Ol Doinyo Lengai Volcano

The Ol Doinyo Lengai volcano is in southern Tanzania, situated on the Great Rift system. This unique volcano sits on a stretch of very contorted country called Sykes Grid. It is believed that Sykes Grid is a very thin part of the Earth's crust because it contains so many hot springs, sulphurous steam jets and other volcanic forms.

Ol Doinyo Lengai is conically shaped and from a distance it appears to be snow-capped, although in fact its sugary crust is due to the chemical constituents of its emissions. Ol Doinyo Lengai is 2,856 metres (9,365 feet) high and it is most famous for its dramatic eruption of ash and sodium carbonate lavas in 1955.

Ol Doinyo Lengai is unusual because its eruptions are alkaline in content, and therefore rich in sodium and deficient in silica, which is the more common major constituent of volcanic lavas. The result is that this abundance of sodium has to combine with whatever it can and so Ol Doinyo Lengai erupts lavas of ash and sodium carbonate, producing what one could almost describe as volcanic soap flakes.

Ol Doinyo Lengai is described as 'gently' active, but Tanzania also boasts Africa's highest mountain, Kilimanjaro, and there are hints that this ancient volcano could be warming up again. Kilimanjaro is only three degrees south of the Equator and astonishingly there are still glaciers on her heights. But the rainfall on the great mountain's summit is only about 20 centimetres (8 inches) a year which is not enough to keep pace with the amount of ice lost annually through melting. It is estimated that Kilimanjaro's glaciers will not last indefinitely and possibly only for another two hundred years. The mountain's increased volcanic activity could be raising the temperature further and thus accelerating the disappearance of Kilimanjaro's unlikely glaciers.

Northern Tanzania also contains the largest volcanic crater in the world. The immense Ngorongoro crater is 311 square kilometres (120 square miles) in area and it has probably been extinct for about a quarter of a million years. Today its floor is a luxuriant pasture-land and a national park exists to protect the sometimes

Right: Ol Doinyo Lengai's crater, famous for its dramatic eruptions of ash and sodium carbonate lavas.

conflicting interests of the Masai tribes who still live there and the teeming wild-life.

The roguish and still lively Ol Doinyo Lengai volcano is situated on the southern edge of a remarkable lake which consists of layers of crystalline sodium carbonate overlying extremely evil-smelling black mud and it is a very shallow lake. This is Lake Natron, the home of thousands of exotic flamingos who live there for a combination of reasons. The soda-saturated water suits their feeding habits, and in the stinking mud-flats of the lake's centre they nest in their thousands. In the middle of the noisome, scorching lake they are safe from greedy predators, ranging from the vulture to the lion who greatly crave flamingo suppers. The young and vulnerable flamingos do not leave the centre of the lake until they can fly. Until then they exist as a dash of pink on a brownish blur in the middle of white soda water, while above them soars the truly phenomenal Ol Doinyo Lengai volcano.

The Trinidad Pitch Lake

This extraordinary lake is one of the least lovely sights in an otherwise beautiful island. Despite this it is Trinidad's most famous feature. It is not unique as there is a similar lake in nearby Venezuela and some asphalt pits in California, but it is certainly the most renowned example of a strange phenomenon and it is perhaps the largest deposit of asphalt in the world. The contents of the Lake are a mix of 40 per cent bitumen, 30 per cent colloidal clay and 30 per cent salt-water and the mixture is remarkably uniform and consistent in all parts of the lake. The strange, dark surface of the gloomy pool covers 44 hectares (109 acres) and its slimy contents plummet to a maximum depth of 82 metres (271 feet).

As an ordinary lake has ripples, the Pitch Lake has folds and almost stationary waves. In the rainy season the hollows between the folds collect pools of water. The whole mass of asphalt is in a continual state of mild ferment and, although the surface is solid enough to walk on, it occasionally bubbles and plops as sulphurated gas forces its way out. This sinister, grey-black stew is surprisingly dotted with islands of vegetation, for wherever wind-blown leaves and other vegetation form a pocket of compost in the folds, scrub trees germinate, sink their roots into the asphalt and grow to a height of about four metres (15 feet). The Lake has been quarried for its contents for over 100 years but shows few scars as the asphalt soon oozes back into any trench that is dug and fills it up.

A clue to the origins of the Pitch Lake comes from the knowledge that its asphalt contains sea fossils and shells. The rotting remains of these marine animals, which lived 50 million years ago, formed the hydrocarbons which then migrated through permeable rocks. Over the ages rock movements in the Earth's crust forced the oil up some 1219 metres (4,000 feet) to its present position and also saw the removal of the lighter fractions of the oil from the heavy bitumen. Finally the sun played on the exposed surface of bitumen and hardened it to a crust. Convection currents within the Lake cause the slow but continuous movement of the pitch from the centre towards the edges.

Asphalt, bitumen and pitch are all fairly broadly defined and can be used to describe the contents of Trinidad's Lake. Naturally occurring, viscous oil-based substances have been found and used since the earliest civiliza-

Right: The Pitch Lake's fascination lies in its strange and gloomy consistency rather than natural beauty as it is normally understood.

tions. Archaeologists have discovered that the Sumerians used them as a cement and the Babylonians employed them to give a good, waterproof surface to pavements, stairways and baths. Since then they have been continuously in use in a variety of ways. The Trinidad Lake must have been discovered by Europeans soon after Columbus visited the island but it does not appear in written records until 1595. At that time Sir Walter Raleigh, the quarrelsome English fortune-hunter, colony-founder and purveyor of tobacco and potatoes, paused at Trinidad to burn and sack its capital, St Jose de Oruna. Sir Walter noted 'at this point called Tierra de Brea or Piche, there is that abundance of stone pitch that all the shippes of the world may be therewith laden from thence, and we made triall of it in trimming our shippes to be most excellent good and melteth not in the sunne as Pitche of Norway. . .'. The commercial development of the Lake, however, had to wait until the end of the nineteenth century.

The Pitch Lake is valuable as well as strange. An apparently inexhaustible asset, it forms a contrast to the rest of a delightful tropical island – although only an improbable geological chance brought it into existence.

Black Sand

A black beach provides an unusual, interesting and barely credible sight. There is a delightful richness of contrasting colours as the green or blue waves surge up the dark background of the beach while foam and sea spray provide a thick, creamy border at the water's edge. The black sands themselves often have unexpected qualities; dark sands absorb heat far more readily than lighter sands which reflect it, so that a sunny day can turn a barefoot romp over black sand into a scramble for the soothing coolness of the sea. Some black-sand beaches, when dry, emit sounds when walked upon. The so-called barking sands of Kauai in the Hawaiian islands are well renowned for being noisy underfoot. Singing sands, as they may be termed, are not confined, however, to the black varieties and, indeed, most of us have been able to extract a small squeak from dense, dry, packed, white sand as we trample over it. The whole question of obtaining some sort of sound reaction from sand depends upon its texture which, in turn, must depend upon its origins.

In the most general terms one can say that black sands are more common on the shores of oceanic islands than on mainland beaches. There are plenty of exceptions to this general rule – particularly on the Australian coast – but it holds good in the majority of cases. The reason for this is that the sand found on the beaches of any land is usually the product of the erosion of that land and continental land masses are normally composed of different rocks from those which form oceanic islands. As oceanic islands are generally produced by volcanic action, they are made up of black basaltic lavas, which are devoid of the hard mineral quartz. In contrast, continental lands are composed of a whole variety of volcanic and sedimentary rocks which overall contain a significant content of quartz. Because of its abundance, hardness and chemical resistance, it is quartz which normally withstands the process of erosion and so breaks down into comparatively large sand-sized particles – while the other minerals are broken down to smaller particles of silt or mud which are easily washed out to sea. As a result the sandy beaches of continents are usually made up of fine-grained quartz which produces the familiar lighter sands.

On oceanic islands, beach materials are different. The erosion of coral or shells can give sparkling white beaches to atolls and islands protected by barrier reefs. In other cases the black basalt provides fragments which fringe the shore with black or greenish beaches. Even so black sands are not common despite the countless islands which litter the oceans. Some of the most spectacular black shores occur as a result of unique circumstances. Iceland boasts many dramatic black beaches which are composed of volcanic ash. Volcanic ash is the product of an explosive eruption and the fragments are roughly similar in size to grains of sand. Eruptions from some of Iceland's many volcanoes have formed huge banks of ash on the seashore where it is further refined by the pounding of the waves. Different again are some of the beaches of New Zealand and Australia, far from active volcanoes, where black minerals have been eroded from the rocks of the land and, by means of odd current actions, have accumulated in high proportions in some of the beach sands. A few of these beaches are even quarried for the metal value of the minerals.

Right: The black sand which gives such picturesque qualities to this Icelandic beach is composed of volcanic ash which has been refined by breaking waves.

Further Reading

BARDARSON, H. R. *Ice and Fire* (H. R. Bardarson, Reykjavik, 1972)

BARRY, R. G. and CHORLEY, R. J. *Atmosphere, Weather and Climate* (Methuen, London, 1971; Holt, Rinehart & Winston, New York, 1970)

CLOUDSLEY-THOMPSON, J. *The Desert* (Orbis Publishing, London, 1977; G. P. Putnam's, New York, 1977)

DYSON, J. L. *The World of Ice* (Cresset Press, London, 1963)

FRASER, C. *The Avalanche Enigma* (J. Murray, London, 1966; Rand McNally, Chicago, 1966)

GASS, I. G. (Ed.) *Understanding the Earth* (Artemis Press, Horsham, 1972; M.I.T. Press, Cambridge, Mass., 1973)

HAGEN, T. *et al. Mount Everest* (Oxford University Press, Oxford, 1963)

MATTHEWS, W. H. *The Story of Volcanoes and Earthquakes* (Harvey House, Irvington on Hudson, New York, 1969)

OJAKANGAS, R. and DARBY, D. G. *The Earth: Past and Present* (McGraw-Hill, New York, 1976)

PILKINGTON, R. *The Ways of the Sea* (Routledge & Kegan Paul, London, 1968)

POWELL, J. W. *The Exploration of the Colorado River and its Canyons* (University of Chicago Press, Chicago, Illinois, 1973)

STERLING, T. *The Amazon* (Time-Life International 1974)

TOSCO, U. *Exotic Flowers and Trees* (Orbis Publishing, London, 1975; Bounty Books, New York, 1975)

WALTHAM, A. C. *The World of Caves* (Orbis Publishing, London, 1976; G. P. Putnam's, New York, 1976)

Acknowledgements

We are grateful to the following for permission to reproduce illustrations on pages:

7 NASA; 9 J. R. Wooldridge; 10–11 P2; 12–13 N. Cirani; 14–15 N. Cirani/IGDA; 16 Ostman; 17 N. Cirani; 18–19 Ardea/Peter Steyn; 20–21 R. Cassin; 22–23 Doug Scott; 25 N. Cirani/IGDA; 26–27 N. Cirani/IGDA; 27 (top) N. Cirani/IGDA; 28 N. Cirani/IGDA; 31 Foto V. Radnicky; 32 A. C. Waltham; 33 A. C. Waltham; 34 A. C. Waltham; 34–35 Spectrum; 35 (top) A. C. Waltham; 37 (top) Photo Loic-Jahan; 37 (bottom) A. C. Waltham; 39 (top) Explorer/Jacques Trotignon; 39 (bottom) Giorgio Gualco; 40–41 N. Cirani; 43 Zefa; 44–45 US Geological Survey – Eros Data Center; 46–47 B. Plossu; 49 Ardea; 50–51 Ardea/K. W. Tink; 52–53 Picturepoint; 54–55 Pictor; 57 IGDA; 58–59 J. Six; 61 Keystone; 62–63 D. Washington/ Bruce Coleman; 64 Marka; 65 Marka/Bavaria Verlag; 66–67 A-Z Botanical; 68–69 P2; 70–71 N. Cirani; 72 N. Cirani; 73 N. Cirani; 75 M. Fantin; 77 Robert Harding; 78–79 Werner Forman Archive; 80 A. C. Waltham; 81 A. C. Waltham; 82 Bruce Coleman/W. E. Ruth; 82–83 A. C. Waltham; 85 Swissair; 87 Bruce Coleman/C. Bonnington; 88 Explorer/S. Bougaeff; 89 IGDA; 90 Robert Harding/F. Jackson; 92–93 Pictor/Starfoto; 95 N. Cirani; 96 Explorer/ J. Thomas; 97 Pictor; 98–99 Pictor; 101 Ardea/Taylor; 102–103 F. Quilici; 105 Time-Life; 107 IGDA; 108–109 Robert Harding/Sassoon; 111 N. Cirani; 112–113 Bruce Coleman/F. Eritz; 114–115 Beaujard-Cedri-Titus; 116–117 ZFA/Pictor; 117 (top) G. Mazza; 117 (bottom) G. Mazza; 118–119 Bill Mason; 120 N. Cirani; 121 N. Cirani; 122–123 Robert Harding; 124–125 Pictor; 125 Spectrum; 127 C. M. Dixon; 128–129 Bill Mason; 130 Picturepoint; 130–131 Bill Mason; 131 Peters; 132–133 SEF; 133 M. E. Parker; 134 The Meteorological Office; 135 J. H. Golden; 136–137 F. Lane/Wayne C. Carlson; 138–139 (top) Daily Telegraph/ C. Bonnington; 138–139 (bottom) IGDA; 140 Marka; 142–143 Bruce Coleman/D. Sahdev; 143 (top) NASA/IGDA; 145 NASA/IGDA; 147 (top) Jack Novak; 147 (bottom) Orbis Publishing; 148–149 Orbis Publishing; 151 ICP; 153 Picturepoint; 154–155 Orion Press; 156 Marka; 157 IGDA; 158 IGDA/G. Tomsich; 159 IGDA/T. Miček; 161 Daily Telegraph; 162–163 Pubbli-Aer-Foto; 165 Vulcain-Explorer; 166 Orbis Publishing; 167 Titus; 168 Bruce Coleman; 169 N. Cirani; 170 Titus; 171 Titus; 172–173 Icelandic Photo & Press Service; 175 L. Lee Rue/ Bruce Coleman; 176–177 Bruce Coleman/G. D. Plage; 178–179 Vulcain-Explorer; 181 IGDA/SEF; 182–183 Bruce Coleman; 185 Spectrum; 187 P2.

Index